THE LATE TEENAGE YEARS

THE LATE TEENAGE YEARS

From seventeen to adulthood

*Luis Rodriguez de la Sierra and
Joan Schachter*

KARNAC

First published in 2013 by
Karnac Books Ltd
118 Finchley Road
London NW3 5HT

British Library Cataloguing in Publication Data

A C.I.P. for this book is available from the British Library

ISBN-13: 978-1-78049-180-6

Typeset by V Publishing Solutions Pvt Ltd., Chennai, India

Printed in Great Britain

www.karnacbooks.com

CONTENTS

SERIES EDITOR'S FOREWORD

When focusing on an individual aged between seventeen and twenty-three, how can one decide whether to think of him[1] as a late adolescent or as a young adult? Perhaps, from a legal point of view it is enough to establish his date of birth, but from a psychological viewpoint and, even more complex, from an experiential point of view, this is a very difficult decision to make.

Before embarking on clinical work with a person in late adolescence, the psychodynamic professional will need to assess his subject's degree of emotional maturity, but he must never neglect to take into account the social circumstances of the individual. If the youngster lives in his parents' home and depends on their financial and emotional support, this will influence his approach to peers and to society in general, whatever the level of his emotional maturity.

Dr Rodriguez de la Sierra and Dr Schachter have produced a clear and detailed description of the challenges that the late adolescent has to face through the years of his progress from adolescence into adulthood. The professional reader should find very helpful their analysis of the various pathological issues that clinical practice presents. Dr Rodriguez de la Sierra has included in this book the text of one of his lectures to practising therapists and counsellors, where he discusses the challenges, frustrations, and gratifications that the work with these most difficult patients can present.

The literature describing the developmental stages that lead the infant into adulthood contains two aspects that deserve to be made explicit and discussed. One is the difference between references to the *actual* infant, as distinct from those focusing on the *reconstructed* infant (Stern, 1995); the other follows on from this and involves the degree of experience that the authors have of direct, close involvement with infants and children. It is very easy to ignore these features, but, once aware of them, one realises their importance and the degree to which they affect the views expressed.

Over the years, I have met many analysts and psychotherapists in order to discuss the observation of infants or actual clinical work with children. I have come to recognise that some of these students or qualified professionals speak about the infant or child they are involved with in a manner that suggests a sense of distance and coldness; they seem to be reporting the finding of something they have read or heard about. I cannot pick up that tone of delight and warmth that is experienced when discovering something new in an object that one feels close to, the sense of excitement and discovery aroused when an individual object is approached from a background of recognition and familiarity. In other words, having had the experience of being close to other infants or children, there is the gratifying discovery that this is not "just another infant", but a new, different, special infant, with his own, unique characteristics.

Eventually, it occurred to me to ask these students what previous experience they had with young children and I was surprised to find that the infant they observed, or the child they were treating, was the first child they had ever come so close to. These were professionals who had trained to work with adults, and it became clear that the images they had of an "infant" or a "child" had been gained from their studies. I later found out that most people who decide to train in the analytic approach to children opt for the child psychotherapy training, while those who choose the psychoanalytic training aim to work with adults. This may well be the explanation for the failure of all the efforts made by so many analysts to persuade their trainees to get involved with children or, at least, with the study of children.

Anna Freud (1972) saw the child as a live field of research and she believed that "child analysis … opened up the possibility to check up on the correctness of reconstructions in adult analysis" (p. 153). And yet,

> analysts of adults remained more or less aloof from child analysis, almost as if it were an inferior type of professional occupation … . It was difficult not to suspect that most analysts vastly preferred the childhood images which emerged from their interpretations to the real children in whom they remained uninterested. (p. 153)

Hannah Segal (1972) shared Anna Freud's views:

> In our institute in Great Britain we had for years lectures on child analysis and clinical seminars, which were compulsory for all students. Unfortunately, we are going through one of our periodic great upheavals and reorganization, and I find to my horror that the child has been thrown out with the bath water: the course of child analysis for the ordinary candidate has disappeared, I hope only very temporarily. (p. 160)

To help a professional to obtain a true and through familiarity with the growing child, she listed what she saw as her

> minimal requirements: first, full integration of theory
> of psychoanalytic knowledge derived from the analysis
> of children in teaching; secondly, baby and child obser-
> vation; and thirdly, attendances at lectures and clinical
> seminars on child analysis irrespective of whether the
> candidate is treating children himself. (p. 160)

In fact, infant observation is the only one of these disciplines
that has been (virtually) universally adopted as part of the
training in adult analysis and psychotherapy. However, analysing the reports of students and reading the available literature, we can recognise the effect of the preconceptions with
which the observers approach infant and parent(s). We can
only *see* what *we make* of that which our eyes show us. This is
not pathological; it is an inevitable fact. Whichever one of our
senses is stimulated, some perception is formed and immediately interpreted in line with previous experience. Presumably,
each of us is able to spot a sensorial stimulus not previously
met, but while some stop and try to make sense of it, others
quickly ignore it, choosing to concentrate on more familiar
perceptions and interpretations. Of course, nobody reaches
adulthood without having been involved with children of all
ages, but there is a major difference between taking an interest,
developing a relationship, and warming up to children and,
on the other hand, approaching children as no more than an
object of study.

Friends, colleagues, acquaintances, relatives of all ages
arouse feelings and images of various degrees of clarity in
our minds and we are usually able to describe their quali-
ties and attributes as individuals. But on becoming a student,
there is a powerful qualitative change in our frame of mind
and we move on to learn and search for group characteristics; indeed, this is a response to what most teachers expect
from their trainees. In zoology we learn of species, races,
genders, etc., much as in psychology we discover all kinds of

classifications of appearance, behaviours, etc. Since medicine has "diagnosis" as the primary goal in its process of investigation of the individual patient, the student has to work hard to learn the relevant data to consider when making his "differential diagnosis", that is, having considered all *possible* illnesses that *might* be affecting that particular individual, deciding which one is, in fact, producing the specific clinical phenomena he presents.

And here lies the problem I want to define and focus on. Meeting an infant or a child we are flooded with images and possible interpretations of what *that* child's appearance, behaviour, utterances, etc. are supposed to indicate. But having examined each and every one of these *impressions*, we still have to admit that these are no more than interpretations based on our previous life experiences. Only a closer interaction with the particular child will help us to clarify which of our hypotheses are, in fact, correct—and, at last, recognise and define the specific cluster of conscious and unconscious thoughts and emotions experienced by the child that leads to his manifest behaviour and utterances.

The reports of students on their observations of infants demonstrate very clearly the degree to which their descriptions reflect the theoretical framework in which they are being trained. Indeed, their *personal* opinions also influence what they perceive, and only when they give a detailed enough description of their observations will other students be able to recognise other possible ways of interpreting what has been observed. Two examples may illustrate this point:

> A seven-month-old baby was described as particularly unresponsive to the mother's ministrations. The student, in fact, at times considered the mother's behaviour as a possible cause of the baby's responses. Taking a broader view of the three visits under discussion, the other students in the group questioned the assessment of their

colleague. After some discussion, it occurred to me to ask whether he might be considering the baby's behaviour as an early sign of autism—rather hesitantly he admitted this was the case. This led to a major change in the focus of the discussion. Subsequent visits led to reports of a baby developing normally, with a mother who seemed to treat him in a very normal manner.

A ten-week-old baby was described as "attacking the mother's nipple in an oral sadistic" manner and, accordingly, producing pain and a withdrawal reaction in the mother. When the student visited the family the following week, the baby was reported as sucking quite normally at the mother's breast. The students in the group were, obviously, puzzled and asked about the destructive oral instincts of the baby—the reporting student, rather timidly, answered that the mother had been visited a few days earlier by a breastfeeding counsellor.

As infants learn to speak and to convey their feelings in a more understandable manner, it becomes easier to make contact with them and gradually learn to understand how they are experiencing life in the world around them. But, predictably, this is easier said than done. Parents, teachers, doctors, find it much easier to *tell* the child what they think, than to find a way of enabling the child to express what, in fact, are his experiences. Teaching, reassuring, ignoring, comforting, pacifying—or punishing—a child is infinitely easier than conveying to that child that one is interested in discovering what is exciting, worrying, bothering, or frightening him or her.

The parents of a twelve-year-old boy were worried by his behaviour, his refusal to discuss anything with them. School reports were satisfactory, but the parents worried that the boy might be developing some kind of pathological aloofness. I saw the boy on his own and found no sign of the behaviour reported by the parents. I suggested to the parents that I should meet the boy a few more times, but I reassured them that I had not detected any indication of incipient pathology in their son. I wondered whether the behaviour at home might be a pattern developed within the child's relationship with the parents and inquired what image they had of their interactions with the boy in his earlier years. After some thought, the father recounted that, one day, when he was four years old, the boy had told him that he "knew that God created the earth". Father had said that this was good and had continued doing what he was involved with. But, after a few minutes, the boy asked him: "Do you want me to tell you how it is that I know?" The father felt embarrassed, and asked the boy to tell him. "Because there was no ground for anyone to stand on, so only a God could have done it". I suggested that this episode might have remained in the boy's mind as a warning that, in principle, his father was not interested in learning about his thoughts.

If I had only seen the boy by himself, I would not have heard about this episode. Individual sessions would probably have revealed his inability to feel free and spontaneous when addressing his father and perhaps he might have been helped not to extend this sense of intimidation to his relationship with other men. But if the father can realise the impact his responses have on his son, this may lead him to develop a different pattern of reaction to him. Broadening our picture, we have, here, examples of keeping an open mind when approaching a child and his parents. The student who thought he was observing an autistic child could recognise the extent to which his initial impressions were influencing his subsequent analysis of his data; the student who thought she had found evidence of Klein's theories regarding the destructive aspects of the oral instincts could take into account the subsequent piece of evidence that strongly argued against her interpretation of the baby's behaviour. The memory put forward by the father of the twelve-year-old boy is a powerful piece of evidence of the importance, at all ages, of environmental factors shaping up a child's mode of relating to his environment.

These arguments and examples aim to depict an approach to child development where the emphasis is on the actual personal experience of each child and his parents, rather than on a particular body of theories built to explain human development. We stress the richness and freedom that a sense of doubt can create, rather than on the advocacy of dogmatic certainty. Instead of starting from a theoretical base and searching for the evidence that will substantiate it, we are choosing an approach where we aim to understand the personal experience of the child and of his parents, and gradually build up a picture of the development of their interaction.

The concept of instinctual impulses is well accepted in all areas of biology, but in the analytic world it has become attached to psychoanalytic concepts to an extent that, in my opinion, is difficult to justify. For example the concepts of self and of object images are useful in evaluating the level of development of an infant's ego, but when it is postulated that instincts can influence the formation of object images *in utero*, I consider this the type of hypothesis that demands *faith* for its acceptance, since we do not have the equipment to evaluate its validity. The episode quoted above—of the observer who claimed to have found evidence of how hostile impulses had led an infant to attack its bad maternal object—is an example of this particular application of the concept of inborn instincts.

The opposite extreme is represented by those theories that claim that the infant's personality is the result of the environment in which he grows up. These theories will always include comments on the importance of other factors in shaping the infant's development, but not much notice is given to these "other" factors in the description of the developing infant and child. Predictably, analysts will develop their clinical approach in line with the theoretical framework they favour. For example, analysts who maintain that psychopathology originates from early infancy mothering will see early developmental pathology in the patient's material and, correspondingly, will attempt to offer a more effective mothering experience.

The authors of the books in this series follow a balanced view of these various theories. There is a refreshing lack of dogmatic views and a high dose of good sense, where theories are respected and quoted, always making sure that a reader can find enough material to form his own view on the validity of the interpretations put forward.

Each book in this series focuses on a particular age range of a child's development. The emphasis is on the description of the typical ways in which the child, at each of these stages, experiences himself in his world. As he develops, the child has different needs, abilities, and resources that underlie his interaction with parents, relatives, and the world at large. Our objective is to illustrate how these unfolding characteristics of the child influence, and are influenced by, the people in his world. It is only careful and (usually) long-term observation that will allow us to identify elements in the infant's or child's behaviour that are likely to be part of his inborn personality.

When considering a particular individual, it is not difficult to put forward hypotheses about the origins of his various characteristic features—but the converse is virtually impossible. However refined our powers of observation, we are quite incapable of predicting what effects the course of time will produce on an individual. Here lies the special fascination in studying infants and children, where all the time we are surprised by some piece of behaviour we could not have predicted.

Meeting the child and his parents we have to explore the patterns of the relationship they have with each other, and it is virtually impossible to establish what is cause and what is effect in the way they treat each other. Through their words and behaviour, child and parents continuously confirm each other's expectations and maintain a self-perpetuating vicious circle, where each of them feels totally justified in his/her view of himself/herself and of each other. However, if we find a way of enabling a child to reveal his private thoughts and feelings, we can sometimes discover that these do not quite match his usual statements: most children learn to sense and respect how each parent expects them to behave and what to say, and when and where to say it.

All the authors in this series follow a theoretical framework that maintains the importance of emotional and intellectual factors of which we may be unconscious at a particular time. They also follow the theory that individuals are continuously influenced by their experiences, past and present, both those originating in the person's mind and those resulting from interactions with other people. This approach is referred to as a "dynamic" view of the human personality. However, all our authors are aware of the existence of factors in our make-up that appear not to be amenable to change. In fact, we are privileged in having a specific volume in the series that addresses the issue of disadvantage. Given appropriate professional help, disadvantaged children can improve their capacity to deal with life, but in many cases it will be difficult to predict the extent of change and, equally important, to determine whether the child has acquired new coping mechanisms or, instead, structural changes have been achieved.

These differences are significant, not just from a scientific point of view, but also in terms of what we, the professionals, convey to the parents about our assessment of their child. When a child has a structural, inborn, or acquired problem, we owe it to the parents to acknowledge how, in the course of time, they have learnt of the child's abilities and limitations and have found ways of taking these into account when looking after the child. In other words, that some of the child's problems are the result not of upbringing but of some factor that is not always easy to pinpoint. When there is no physical, organic, non-dynamic factor, we can assume we are facing a dynamic problem, but even then it can be difficult to predict the extent to which our therapeutic efforts will achieve change in the presenting problems. This is, in fact, the most difficult challenge that a consultant faces each time a new child is assessed.

It is quite common that parents will present different readings from each other of what he or she considers the child's problems to be. Needless to say, the same is true when looking at any issue in the life of an ordinary family. The baby cries and the mother thinks he is hungry, while the father may feel that here is an early warning of a child who will wish to control his parents' lives. The toddler refuses some particular food and the mother resents this early sign of rebellion, while the father will claim that the child is actually showing he can discriminate between pleasant and undesirable flavours. The five-year-old demands a further hour of TV-watching and the mother agrees he should share a programme she happens to enjoy, while the father explodes at the pointlessness of trying to instil a sense of discipline in the house. By the time the child reaches puberty or adolescence, these clashes are a matter of daily routine. From a practical point of view, it is important to recognise that there is no question of ascertaining which parent is right or which one is wrong: within their personal frames of reference, they are both right. The problem with such disagreements is that, whatever happens, the child will always be agreeing with one of them and opposing the other. But at this point I wish to emphasise the obvious fact that each parent reaches his interpretation of the child's behaviour in line with his upbringing and his personality, his view of himself in the

world, his past and present experiences, some of them conscious, most of them unconscious. But what about the child in
question?

It is not part of ordinary family life that a child should be
asked what *his* explanation is for the piece of behaviour that
led to the situation where the parents have disagreed on its
interpretation. And, anyway, if he *is* asked, there is a fair chance
that, very quickly, one or both parents will challenge him and
utter the famous lines: "Really? I know your antics! Pull the
other one! What you really wanted is …". It is just not common
to find parents (or even adults in general) who are interested
in, and able to discover, the private justification a child might
have for his behaviour. Sometimes, the child fails to find the
words to explain himself, occasionally he is driven to say what
he believes the parent wants to hear; at other times his words
sound too illogical to be believed—somehow the myth has
grown that only a professional has the capacity to fathom the
child's motives and intentions.

Each family will have its own style of approaching their
child. It is simply unavoidable that each individual child will
have his development influenced (note: not determined, but
affected) by the responses his behaviour brings out in his
parents. It is, however, quite difficult for parents to appreciate the precise developmental abilities achieved by their
child. No child can operate, cope with life, respond to stim-
uli, beyond his particular abilities at any particular point in
time. And this is *the* point addressed in the present series of
books. We try to paint a portrait of the various stages in the
child's cognitive, intellectual, emotional development and
how these unfolding stages affect not only his experience
of himself, but also how he perceives and responds to the
world in which he lives. We hope that this approach will help
parents and professionals to gauge how best to make contact
with the child and to reach an understanding of his feelings
and behaviour.

References

Freud, A. (1972). Child analysis as a sub-speciality of psychoanalysis. *International Journal of Psychoanalysis*, 53: 151–156.

Segal, H. (1972). The role of child analysis in the general psychoanalytical training. *International Journal of Psychoanalysis*, 53: 157–161.

Stern, D. (1995). *The Motherhood Constellation*. New York: Basic Books.

Note

1. For the sake of simplicity we will use *he, his*, and *him* whenever both genders are referred to.

INTRODUCTION

Adolescence is the process, both psychic and physical, which organises and integrates the changes initiated by puberty. The first manifestations of the capacity to procreate (first period for girls, first emission for boys) may commence the process of adolescence but, in some cases, the psychological changes may start earlier. How these changes are experienced by the child may determine whether adolescence is first experienced in a bodily way or not. The connection between puberty and adolescence is obvious, but it is important to differentiate the two processes.

With the arrival of puberty, Freud tells us, "… changes set in which are destined to give infantile sexual life its final and normal shape" (1905, p. 207). Before puberty the sexual life of the child is predominantly autoerotic, that is, centred mostly on the child's own body, but the arrival of puberty leads to a sexual interest in others. In the last thirty years puberty in girls has tended to start earlier, namely at the age of nine or ten, rather than between twelve and fourteen, the reasons for which are not yet well known. The age of puberty in boys has become later, similarly for reasons as yet unknown. As this series of books indicates, we consider adolescence as being divided roughly into three periods: early, from twelve to fifteen; middle, from fifteen to seventeen; and late, from seventeen to twenty-one. These three periods can be quite different in their nature. The early and middle phases are particularly difficult, not only for the young person but also for his or her family, because of the seemingly abrupt changes which occur in the young adolescent under the impact of the biological developments.

A real difficulty arises when we try to define the end of adolescence, an end that seems to have become less clearly defined and more prolonged in recent years. Since the sexual and social revolution of the 1960s, it is increasingly less clear what an adolescent is expected to be and to have achieved. In theory we know that the end of the adolescent process coincides with the moment when the transformation of various identifications leads to the acquisition of a stable, well-established personal and sexual identity. These new identifications must include the accepted social code as part of the new independent identity and status, which ceases to need or rely upon parental protection.

If all goes well, the end of adolescence occurs around the age of eighteen to twenty-one, but if there is a foreclosure of the adolescent process, or if it is short-circuited, the adolescent will not be able to achieve the necessary independence and will be unable to fully accept his sexually mature body. By this we mean that some aspects of identity may be foreclosed. Foreclosure occurs when the adolescent makes an allegiance to some aspect of identity without having had the chance to explore other alternatives; for instance, a premature sexual, ideological, religious, or occupational "choice" which has been made under stress and without having had the opportunity to experiment or investigate other possibilities. These "choices" often originate in the ideas and beliefs of adults, peers, or certain "politicised" sections of society, which are accepted without question. We refer here to some social doctrines which are often proclaimed with passion, but where the degree of primitive fantasy that informs them goes unrecognised, which makes them all the more powerful. There is nothing more dangerously impervious to argument than a strong conviction of unknown origin, whose wish-fulfilling force exerts to the full the powers of rationalisation on those who pursue what they take to be adult liberation at all costs. A commitment to such ideas, made by a vulnerable adolescent, is often the origin of what we mean by foreclosure of the adolescent process.

In this short book we would like to show the different ways in which a problematic end to the adolescent process may manifest itself. Sometimes this is evident and we are confronted by severe psychological illness, whilst in other individuals the incomplete end of the adolescent process is disguised by defences which appear to be adaptive but, in fact, interfere with development. It is not always easy in this phase of development to differentiate transient problems from those that will become persistent. Individuals mature at different rates, and cultural and familial factors have also to be taken into account when trying to understand the concerns of the adolescent and his parents.

Late adolescence is characterised by a resolution of earlier conflicts that facilitates the consolidation of personal and sexual identity and leads to the achievement of true independence and autonomy. However, as we shall discuss, for some adolescents this is not always the case. We may find a persistence of unresolved conflicts which continue to produce friction with adults and the beginning of the development of "undesirable" traits. This could be associated with a delay in moving on to adulthood. We are talking here about the common problems of sexual orientation, professional decisions, and the increasing problem that young people find nowadays in achieving financial independence.

Though we have in this series of short books divided adolescence into three phases, adolescent development needs to be seen as a continuum in which a wide range of behaviour, attitudes, and actions can be observed, where normality and pathology easily overlap, producing confusion both in the parents and in the adolescents. The significance of the behaviour and attitudes depends to some extent on the age at which they occur and on the family context, therefore different measures will be required from parents and/or professionals. These factors must be taken into account when assessing or trying to understand the adolescent in question.

The problems which the individual has to deal with in adolescence are qualitatively different from those of childhood; they are related in particular to the adolescent's reaction/ responses to the physical development of his sexual body, and to the changing relationship to the parents and to the world in which he lives. In summary, we have to take into account the revival of infantile conflicts and the newly emerging sexual and aggressive urges and experiences, both of which have to be integrated by the adolescent so that a new equilibrium can be created. The adolescent finds himself in the very difficult position of having to make all these readjustments whilst dealing with the subsequent conflicts and anxieties. The earlier passionate mixture of love and hatred that characterises attachment and dependency on the parents must now be renounced until the adolescent reaches a point at which it is possible for him to confirm his own identity and find new love relationships. These must neither be based too much on repetition of previous early attachments nor entirely and exaggeratedly opposed to them. It goes without saying that none of this can be achieved without much upheaval and experimenting.

Some of the major problems that can appear in late adolescence may be directly linked to earlier developmental failures in which difficulties have undergone a process of false resolution: this may lead to a foreclosure of adolescent development, with serious repercussions in later life. A persistence of unresolved conflicts may continue to produce friction with adults and the beginning of the consolidation of "undesirable" traits, causing anxiety both in the adolescent and in the adults. We may also see what appears to be an endless continuation of adolescence well into the late twenties. Because adolescents have to attempt to break away from parental attachments and constraints, they try to replace these with new attachments to their peers and to other role models which are provided by perhaps less threatening, more attractive, young adult figures under whose influence they easily fall. The results of this are unpredictable, although we must never forget that good early experiences will have a lifelong influence towards stability. It is always difficult to ascertain from the perspective of behaviour alone whether a particular problem is a sign of transient difficulty and therefore in the process of being overcome, or whether a more serious problem is developing. Adolescence is normally a period of turmoil; sometimes apparent disturbances in adolescence are a sign of health rather than a sign of illness. Placidity in adolescence is not normal; rather it can sometimes suggest a worrying avoidance of conflict, a failure of the adolescent process, and a predisposition for later problems to emerge, such as a breakdown at university.

Although by the end of late adolescence society may expect that most of the familiar adolescent conflicts will be over, this is often far from true. In fact, the transition from adolescence to adulthood is arduous and complicated. Parental concerns about teenage boys and girls are mostly connected to academic achievement, the consolidation of independent functioning, sexual orientation, and the choice of peer relationships. Issues surrounding the risk of pregnancy for girls, and for boys, are a major concern. However, as in earlier phases of adolescence, the parents' concerns may be different in quality and intensity between those they hold for boys and for girls: for boys these concerns may focus on professional development and academic achievement; this is also the case for girls, but the risk of pregnancy is also a cause for concern.

CHAPTER ONE

Normality and pathology in adolescence

The subject of this chapter presents us with a problem, as it is very difficult to state at any stage of adolescence what is normal and what is not, and this does not change during the last phases of this process. The question of what is right and what is wrong during this developmental stage continues to be a controversial one. In this chapter, therefore, we want merely to try to facilitate an understanding of what could be considered normal and abnormal developments, as well as to suggest some basic and necessary criteria for the assessment and comprehension of the main aspects of mental and emotional functioning during this phase of life.

To begin with, the classical stages no longer seem to apply; we now see a prolongation of adolescence well beyond the age limits which were usual until recently. For family and social reasons young people take longer to leave home and, therefore, to achieve one of the most important tasks of the last stages of adolescence: the physical as well as emotional separation and independence from the parents. On the other hand, with the greater sexual freedom that adolescents now enjoy, and under the pressures of certain politicised sections of society, we sometimes see what we call a foreclosure of the adolescent process, particularly when the sexually confused young person unconsciously and prematurely chooses a perverse solution. This may be difficult to assess but we must recognise it, because of its prognostic indications and because of the implications and risks of a fixed perverse development, whatever this perverse development might be.

We often witness the oscillation of public and professional opinion which is unable to decide if a particular piece of adolescent behaviour is to be trivialised and seen as just a passing phase or if it is to be considered exaggerated and seen as pathological. What is important to bear in mind is that periods of crisis are an integral part of the adolescent years. This is a very complex developmental stage and phases of turmoil are an essential part of it as well as evidence of the psychic work that is taking place in the service of that development. The last stages of adolescence are no exception to this rule. We should not assume, though, that everything is part of such crisis without investigating what happens, so that we can make a proper diagnosis and subsequently recommend the appropriate therapy if necessary. A misunderstood and disillusioned adolescent in the last stages of this developmental process is very much at risk of choosing addictions, unconsciously determined teenage pregnancies, or other self-destructive behaviour, including suicide, as possible solutions to what is taking place. Adults—not only parents but also teachers, general practitioners, other medical doctors and nurses, policemen, probation officers, etc.—must be aware of any signs of what we have just mentioned in order to help and prevent a dangerous situation. Needless to say, professional guidance and consultation must be made available to the general public, both adults and adolescents.

Once again we must remember that what happens at all stages of adolescence is specific to the developmental process and is different from what takes place during childhood and later on during adulthood. It is important to bear this in mind, as the older adolescent may resemble the young adult, but in reality he has not yet reached that new stage. While normal adolescence involves periods of emotional turmoil, it is expected that towards the end of adolescence such crises might have been resolved or be in the process of resolution. It is at this stage that we can see and assess the outcome of the process and how the adolescent finally reacts to such outcome. Adolescence is the time of life that culminates in the transition to adult sexuality. Normally one would expect in this last period of adolescence that a higher level of organisation and psychic functioning has been reached and that, therefore, greater autonomy and a more solid identity (in all senses of the word) might be observed. Although a sense of flexibility is necessary when assessing a young person at this stage, we would be concerned if frequent regression to earlier modes of functioning were to reappear. A constant and successive alternation between regression and progression, which appears to be blocked by unsolvable obstacles, would be equally worrying at this stage. Regression in itself can be either normal or pathological but towards the end of adolescence it is the capacity to recover from regression that counts.

The defence mechanisms we all use against anxiety, and against other threats coming from our experience of life, should have diminished towards the end of adolescence. Here it is important to distinguish between those that seriously interfere with the capacity to function (massive projective identification, splitting, disavowal) and those that do not and which are more in the service of functionality (repression, displacement, isolation). Projecting undesirable aspects of ourselves onto others, for instance, is the omnipresent defence mechanism in adolescence but it is not, in itself, at any stage, an indicator of normality or pathology. We should, however, see a decrease of the tendency to project during the final phase of adolescence, while a persistence of this defence mechanism must be viewed with concern.

In her unsurpassed description of adolescence Anna Freud (1958) reminds us that it is normal for the adolescent "... to be more idealistic, artistic, generous, and unselfish than he will ever be again ...." While this applies to all phases of adolescence, that idealism should, by now, be accompanied by greater assertiveness and less dependence on both the primary and the new objects, namely parents and peers. At the same time, we should be able to observe at least an attempt by the adolescent to accept and make peace with the denigrated and rejected parents from previous periods. The elation of adolescence, within the concept of greater acceptance of external reality, can be understood along the lines of the rebellion against the limitations of childhood and puberty having been renounced and there being a greater certainty about being able to go forward in life.

An increased capacity to contain affects and conflicts in thoughts and a resulting diminution of impulsive behaviour are also normal at this stage. On the other hand, the adolescent should be capable of action when necessary rather than being paralysed by disturbing fantasies involving sexual and aggressive impulses. In an ideal world we should see a greater adaptation to the realities of life and a decrease of uncontrollable compulsive acts involving the subject or the other, such as abuse of alcohol and drugs, suicide attempts, high-risk behaviour, sexual promiscuity, adolescent pregnancies, running away, overeating or exaggerated fasting, violence, and diverse types of delinquent behaviour. However, because of the prolongation of adolescence that is now occurring, we may not always see, until later on, some of the positive signs we have just mentioned.

Most important of all is the sexual choice made by the adolescent at this stage. Despite present fashions and "progressive" ideas about sexuality, there is no evidence that the persistence of homosexual or bisexual relationships at this stage could be considered as a normal outcome or solution to the adolescent process, but whatever the sexual choice the adolescent has made by now, it should bear the marks of a less unstable ambiguity than before. The presence of sexual conflicts is of course normal at this stage, as it is also normal during later years, but frequent acting upon such conflicts is not. This acting out may take the form of unrestrained gratification or its opposite: rigid repression at the expense of psychic health, the repression represented, at this stage, by a caricature of the ascetic behaviour of some younger adolescents and masterfully described by Anna Freud in *The Ego and the Mechanisms of Defence*.

It is therefore important at this last stage, when seeing a late teenager or someone in his early twenties, to ascertain what stage of development the young person has reached, if the adolescent process is still under way, if it is still going forward, or if it has suffered a deadlock or is under threat of foreclosure.

The body, we must remember, occupies a central position during adolescent development. The adolescent is very concerned with his body and harbours illusions of perfection. Abandoning such ideas of perfection and bisexuality are essential for injecting the body of a man or a woman with libidinal energy. We know that our relationship with our body dictates our relationship to reality because the sensory impressions and lived experience are passed through by the body, which crucially adapts the representation we make for ourselves of the external world. The function we call "reality testing" enables us to differentiate that representation from perception, namely to distinguish what is not real—what is solely within and therefore confined to a representation—from what is real and which also exists externally. In normal development, by the end of adolescence we have given up our Oedipal wishes, even though they continue to exist in the unconscious, and at the same time we have also unconsciously accepted our infantile feelings of impotence and inferiority. This is all within the context of normal reality testing. When this is impaired we are in the presence of a pathological situation, developmentally abnormal in late adolescence, when the individual is unable or unwilling to give up his infantile wishes and omnipotence. Contact with reality, the reality testing we have been talking about, must not be seen just as present or absent; the adolescent needs to be able to adapt to the instability of his contact with reality in the area of sexuality without giving up his sexual life, his imagination, his capacity for daydreaming, his links with the real outside world. It is important for us to detect inhibition that imitates normality but which in fact operates as a defence against unresolved pathological processes. Daydreaming activity represents a certain elasticity vis-à-vis the interplay of repression and the return of the repressed, an interplay which involves an acknowledgment of reality. By the end of adolescence we should normally expect a greater tolerance of the coexistence of dysfunction and functionality. These are the moments when the adolescent questions his reality testing, when he experiences the sensation of earlier experiences being repeated without panicking because, if all goes well, the coexistence of functioning and dysfunction is tolerated, thus making the adolescence less problematic, which is what is expected towards the end of this stage. The older adolescent should now display a greater capacity for tolerating frustration without being assailed by thoughts of vengeance connected, unconsciously, to the frustration produced by the impotence of childhood.

We should also see an increase in normal constructive aggression in the service of progression regarding relationships, work, and studies and a gradual disappearance of destructive aggression expressed as gratuitous violence.

Towards the end of adolescence we should see a greater equilibrium between the investment he normally has in himself, in his body, in his mind, and the interest he takes in the people in his world.

CHAPTER TWO

Depression and anxiety in the older adolescent

Introduction

"Depression and anxiety to some degree are ubiquitous in adolescence and can be regarded as part of normal adolescent development" (Winnicott, 1965).

All adolescents go through phases of depression and anxiety which are evoked predominantly by feelings of uncertainty about their capacity to become autonomous individuals. The sense of uncertainty about the future also contains feelings about the loss of the safety of childhood. The developmental task of becoming an independent individual is related to the process of separating internally and externally from the childhood relationships of dependence on the parents. The adolescent normally needs to find other figures of identification and role models to help him manage his conflicts over dependence, hence the importance of peer relationships, the extended family, and the parents of friends. Continuing conflicts about dependence on parental figures are likely to create feelings of inner distress, which are easily externalised in diverse ways and at different moments; this process can intensify depressive feelings and create a great deal of anxiety about the future. One of the ways in which this may be expressed is through aggressive attacks on the individual's own body, a behaviour which is usually also connected to intense feelings of shame. An alternative mode of expression may be through displacement of these aggressive feelings onto other figures, more often than not parental substitutes, but also peers. This is further complicated by the fact that the adolescent easily displaces not only negative but also positive feelings which can lead to idealisation of others in the external world. To some extent this idealisation is very much part of the early and middle phases of adolescence; for example the preoccupation with pop stars and film stars. But in the later phase of adolescence these idealisations are usually transformed into ambitions and aims which are more related to the individual's interests and capacities.

It is clearly important to identify those individuals for whom the adolescent depressive conflicts, referred to above, may prove overwhelming, leading to chronic depression and withdrawal or social isolation and academic failure. These will be young people who have suffered from emotional or behavioural difficulties in earlier phases of their development. Some of these difficulties may have been identified as warning signs of later problems to come even if they have not been significant enough to warrant psychological intervention. However, if the adolescent's academic work and social relationships do not suffer significantly, his problems may be regarded as not too much of a cause for concern and the depression may be overlooked.

Anxiety may manifest itself in a number of ways, including in obsessional symptoms (e.g., checking and counting) which reflect an externalised need for greater control over inner experience. Phobic symptoms and irrational fears (e.g., of closed or open spaces) may also appear, but this is less common than in early adolescence.

Depression

By depression we mean a disturbance in the mood and behaviour of the adolescent: a significant lowering of mood, with feelings of sadness, lessened energy and interest in others and the outside world, accompanied by irritation and low self-esteem, and an increased tendency to experience frustration usually with himself or herself, though this may be externalised onto the parents. Depression is often accompanied by feelings of shame and a sense of failure, which may, if extreme, lead to thoughts about suicide. In such individuals, suicide may be thought of as a solution to emotional suffering and a sense of isolation from which they believe they will never emerge. Suicide is clearly an act of aggression against themselves and the most obvious expression of the aggression that is inherent in depression. The low self-esteem which is always part of a depressed mood contains hatred turned against those parts of the self perceived as weak, inadequate, and failing. These inner feelings and experiences lead adolescents to isolate themselves. It may be difficult for the parents to know what is going on and to judge how concerned to be, particularly when their efforts to be available and helpful are rejected. The parents may struggle, at times, to differentiate the adolescent who is trying to be independent and needing his or her privacy from one who is withdrawing into an increasingly depressed and hopeless state.

Whilst many adolescents may entertain fleeting thoughts about suicide—and there is a whole genre of romantic literature extolling the virtues of suicide as an act of freedom—persistent thoughts of suicide are always a cause for serious concern meriting professional intervention. Suicidal gestures are not uncommon in adolescence, and should always be taken seriously, however much the adolescent subsequently denies his intention.

When adolescents leave home to go to university, or leave home for the first time, they may become depressed as a result of finding that the experience of being alone is more difficult than they had anticipated and provokes feelings of failure. This may occur particularly when they have been openly very keen to leave home and live outside the parents' orbit, only to find themselves feeling lonely and anxious about making contact with their peers. As we describe elsewhere in this book, the peer group is of great importance in adolescence; it is often through relationships with their peers that adolescents can feel less alone with their struggles and find some shared understanding of their difficulties. When they can no longer sustain contact with their peers they are facing a dangerous situation.

Depression may be thought of as being related to the adolescent's sense of his personal worth, whilst anxiety is more likely to be related to specific aspects of his thoughts or behaviour, for example—sexual preferences and fantasies, worries about the body, anticipated academic failure, or fear of closeness with others, however much this is also longed for. As we have indicated, depression in older adolescents may manifest itself as difficulties leaving home or in a breakdown early on whilst at college or university. The adolescent who is unable to progress from school to work or further study is likely to provoke the attention of their parents, either through overt signs of depression and withdrawal or through rebellious or aggressive behaviour.

> **Alan** was nineteen when his GP referred him for psychological help. He was clearly a very troubled young person; he had been expelled from school when he was seventeen, since when he had been unable to pursue any course of study or work. He was self-medicating with cannabis and other drugs, which lessened his conscious experience of anxiety to some extent and also undermined his awareness of the need for professional help. He had frequent violent fights with his father; he consciously expressed a great deal of contempt for his father who was

doing "a contemptible job" and was not as clever as Alan, but he also conveyed an intense sense of deprivation. Alongside his violent behaviour, it was evident that he was struggling with his sexual identity, apparently feeling more comfortable with homosexual relationships, even if still wishing for a relationship with a girl. Whilst the violence he expressed both verbally and physically seemed to be primarily an expression of his inability to psychologically separate from his parents, the fights with the father were multi-determined; at some level, Alan was trying to provoke his father to violently attack him as well as to provoke some kind of physical contact as a form of containment. Alan found it very difficult to accept his need for help, fearful of being controlled and continually needing to maintain an emotional distance; if he was not in a superior position he felt intolerably inferior and abnormal.

Robert was twenty-one when he was referred for psychotherapy; he had made two suicide attempts, and was extremely depressed and hopeless about continuing his life. In contrast to Alan, he was keen to seek help. In the course of his intensive psychotherapy the roots of his difficulties in his early childhood relationships became apparent. The onset of puberty had intensified his earlier problems in establishing a sense of a separate self; he felt overwhelmed by his aggressive and sexual drives. Whilst he felt invaded by his parents he also felt unable to survive on his own, both of which feelings were a source of intense shame and anxiety. He had increasingly withdrawn from all forms of social contact, as he experienced himself as damaged and potentially damaging, unable to feel in control of his aggressive impulses and desires for intimacy. His aggression, which was provoked by contact with others, was directed at his body in his suicide attempts and his excessive exercising and dieting. Understanding his behaviour and the psychological roots of his difficulties in intensive psychotherapy, gradually led to a lessening of his depression and anxiety and he was able to resume his studies and work.

Anxiety and phobia

Most anxiety in older adolescents is still related to their bodies. The normal bodily changes that occur in adolescence are often a great source of anxiety to the young person, who has to adapt to them without always feeling equipped or prepared to do so and who is "taken by surprise" by some of these changes which are both feared and wanted. They affect boys and girls equally, although their preoccupations are expressed differently. Most of this preoccupation is centred on their sexual bodies but underneath there is a similar anxiety about the aggression accompanying these developments; in general there is, in both boys and girls, a recrudescence of the sexual fantasies and confusions belonging to childhood. Anxiety may be expressed in a variety of forms, from overt concerns about their bodies, their sexual fantasies and preferences, to displacements of such anxieties onto external objects or situations (phobias), or displacements internally in the form of hypochondriacal fears.

Boys look forward to the first signs of adolescent sexuality such as pubic hair, increase in the size of their penis, the beginnings of a moustache, the first wet dreams and ejaculations. There is a physical need for masturbation as an outlet for the intense sexual feelings that are part of normal adolescent development. The affirmation of their masculine identity is usually expressed through masturbation, which can fulfil several needs including the reassurance that their penis is still there and functioning. Associated with this there may be an unconscious conflict about their feminine and passive wishes and it is not uncommon, even in older adolescents, to find, in the course of analytic treatment, the existence of unconscious fantasies of wanting to be a girl. This may be behind phenomena that often confuse doctors, such as unexplained nose bleeding, which may express unconscious wishes to menstruate, abdominal bloating expressing pregnancy fantasies, etc. There is frequently a resurgence of anxiety about losing the newly acquired masculinity. Envy of girls may express some aspects of the underlying conflicts referred to above. This is present not only during the early stages of puberty/adolescence, but also towards the end of it, during the period when the adolescent is struggling to deal with and resolve all these sources of conflict once and for all. A look at modern fashion trends in boys and girls bears witness to this.

> **John**, who is in conflict over his aggression expressed the view that girls and women have an easier life because they do not have to struggle in order to have a social position, to work successfully. In so doing John was expressing his wish to be passive (feminine) because to be active (masculine) felt too dangerous. Although heterosexual, John had an obsessive interest in Marilyn Monroe, his idol and the feminine figure he admired and with whom he strongly identified. This interest, whilst potentially worrying to John and his parents alike, may reflect a transient developmental stage during which the unconscious conflicts about aggressive and sexual wishes are being worked through. Indeed, by early adulthood John was no longer interested in Marilyn Monroe.

Girls are anxious about their developing femininity and many are therefore preoccupied with the size of their breasts and with their genital organs, some of which are inside the body and therefore invisible, provoking a particular anxiety that is different from that of boys. They are often concerned with issues of normality and abnormality and this provokes comparisons and competitiveness with peers and their mothers. They may be worried about the presence of what they see as masculine traits such as any kind of facial and/or body hairiness. Girls may therefore become rather anxious about their capacity to attract boys to the point of becoming sexually promiscuous. Concerns about normality and/or pregnancy may be expressed in anxieties about menstruation. The reality of menstruation impels the girl to become aware of the functioning of her sexual body and this may evoke unresolved conflicts of identification with her mother as a child-bearing woman. In addition, the girl may experience anxieties about having caused bodily damage through masturbation, which again may be connected with feelings associated with her internal body spaces. Concerns about changes in body weight may be related not only to earlier conflicts with the parents but to unconscious fantasies about pregnancy which often increase during the last stages of adolescence. The possibility of parenthood linked to some of these body changes always has to be taken into account in order to understand what is worrying the young person— whether it is realistic or not—particularly during the last stages of adolescence.

Adolescents are normally anxious about their sexuality, and at the same time have to contend with the fact that they may be attracted to people of their own sex and feel compelled to act on it. In most adolescents this is a transitional developmental phase which continues the exploration of their own bodies through physical contact with bodies similar to theirs. If it persists to the end of adolescence this will become a conflict, as by then the adolescent has often come to the point of having made a heterosexual choice of partner. These anxieties about sexual orientation are often the origin of some bullying and other aggressive physical attacks on other young people or adults.

Anxieties about unconscious incestuous feelings are dealt with through aggression and are behind physical attacks on the parents or their substitutes.

Peter, a fifteen-year-old boy whose parents had separated when he was ten and who lived alone with his mother, became increasingly agitated as he entered puberty and adolescence. Peter greatly missed his father and found being alone at home with his mother very difficult to tolerate. By age fourteen he had started hitting his mother in the middle of heated arguments, which both excited and frightened him. In his therapy sessions it slowly emerged that hitting his mother was a defence against incestuous Oedipal feelings that terrified him. The act of hitting his mother both gratified the impulse to touch her body and defended him against intolerable feelings of sexual attraction towards his mother.

If we turn to literature for examples of bullies, there is no better one than Robert Musil's novel *The Confusions of Young Törless* (*Die Verwirrungen des Zöglings Törleß*), an account of what goes on in an upper-class boarding school in Austria in the early 1900s and which is now seen as a prophetic account of what was to happen later in Nazi Germany under Hitler's rule. Shy and intelligent young Törless feels somewhat apart from the rest of his classmates, wondering what his place in the scheme of things is. Then, two of his friends accuse another boy, Basini, of scheming and thievery, but instead of reporting it they decide to take matters into their own hands. Törless witnesses the sadistic sexual degradations through which the accused is put, which only heightens Törless' need to understand things. Unwittingly, he (like the attackers) finds himself physically drawn to Basini, something which he is unable to comprehend but against which he is powerless. It is a dark and disturbing look at how adolescents learn about their place in the world through power, brutality, and sexuality.

Anxieties about sexual intercourse are still present in late adolescence despite the apparent knowledge that young people might have. Boys may remain concerned with the possible damage done to their genitals and with the damage they might inflict during intercourse. Girls are more often afraid of being hurt and damaged during intercourse as well as worried about infections and possible pregnancy.

Hypochondriacal symptoms and concerns range from the normal narcissistic investment in the body to more fixed expressions of unconscious anxieties in the form of physical symptoms and preoccupation with illness. The latter reflects conflicts over aggressive impulses and fears of losing bodily integrity. The adolescent who feels guilty about sexual and aggressive wishes may unconsciously punish himself with persecutory hypochondriacal thoughts. There are adolescents who, without any apparent reason, develop fears of becoming HIV-positive and consequently of dying, thus expressing their need for punishment for deeds committed in fantasy. Concerns about bodily illness and death may reflect the recrudescence of earlier childhood anxieties and conflicts that can, in adolescence, become the focus of depressive or phobic symptoms. More often than not, these hypochondriacal anxieties represent, in a distorted manner, castration anxiety and are sometimes replaced by obsessional symptoms or by obsessive, frightening thoughts.

> **Steven** was seventeen when he was referred to a psychotherapist because of academic underachievement. It soon transpired this was connected to some obsessive thoughts he tried to keep at bay all the time. The one that made him most anxious was his fear of corpses, a fear whose origin was a mystery to him. In the course of treatment the recovery of a memory from childhood showed him that this fear was connected to seeing the naked body of his dead aunt and the sexual excitement that followed. An interest in necrophilia developed shortly afterwards and subsequently had to be warded off by making it into a fear he had to defend against. The main fear was of giving

in to his necrophilic impulses and then being punished
for them.

Some adolescents do not experience these internal sources of
anxiety but instead experience conflict with the external world.
The treatment of these adolescents is different from the treatment of adolescents who do experience internal conflict and
anxiety (see Chapter Five on addiction and delinquency).

External events as a source of anxiety and depression

Towards the end of adolescence young people are in the process of solving many of the unconscious internal conflicts mentioned above in order to establish themselves in the world as
autonomous individuals. Illness of parents, divorce, emigra-
tion, and forced displacement all have a particular impact on
the development of the older adolescent that may interfere
with the individuation process of this phase. The adolescent
becomes very anxious about these external events that compel
him to turn his attention away from his need to become a separate person. This might result in returning to earlier worries
and symptoms which may have the partial aim of provoking
concern both in the young person himself and in his parents
and the other adults he is involved with.

Adolescents need to be able to act in the world and have
experiences in relationships which can mitigate some of their
developmental anxieties. If they cannot act because of the level
and nature of their anxiety, then the anxiety persists and probably intensifies. The fear of the loss of the attachment to the
parents, present throughout adolescence and a major source
of anxiety, may become exacerbated by some of these external events. The adolescent may cease to go forward towards
separating from his parents and finds instead a reason to prolong the infantile parental attachment which then becomes
abnormal. Some adolescents retreat from their sexuality and

instinctual urges (sexual and aggressive) and find refuge in being ascetic. Parents who have difficulties in allowing the adolescent to separate and leave collude with the adolescent in trouble, failing to be aware of the consequences of this interaction; this should always be a source of concern if it persists into later adolescence.

Phobias

A phobia is a form of anxiety. It is the externalisation of an internal fear onto an object or a situation which then becomes identified with the internal fear. The object or the situation is then avoided in an attempt to control the fear of the temptation and the subsequent punishment. There can be phobias of almost anything—snakes, mice, rats, spiders, apples, lifts, stairs, school, etc.—but what is important is to understand that any object or situation may be invested with particular fears.

The most common phobias towards the end of adolescence are agoraphobia (fear of open spaces) and claustrophobia (fear of closed spaces) and are closely related to the adolescent fear of losing control over their sexual and aggressive impulses often being externalised onto the avoided situation.

> **Linda**, an overweight nineteen-year-old girl who could not control her appetite, had occasional dreams of killing those who annoyed her, particularly her parents who often commented on her weight. She felt at ease at home in the company of her family, but after puberty developed intense anxieties about going out on her own. During her psychotherapy sessions it became clearer to Linda and her therapist that these anxieties were related to fears of losing control while on her own and actually acting out her murderous dream. The feared streets were felt as places where she might be seen and caught.

Josh, a nineteen-year-old boy lived alone with his mother after his father's death in a car accident. He struggled with an intense attachment to a mother whom he experienced both as seductive and invasive and shortly afterwards he developed claustrophobic symptoms that prevented him from taking lifts and being in other small spaces. During treatment he presented a telling dream after seeing the film *2001: A Space Odyssey* and being impressed with the images of foetus-like creatures in the film. In the dream he was travelling back in time and had found himself trapped in a small cavity guarded by an old witch. The analysis of the dream threw light on the excitement and fear that accompanied a thinly disguised fantasy of being in his mother's womb thus transformed into a fear of being in closed spaces.

Some adolescents will use counter-phobic measures to defend against the feared situation.

Adam was an eighteen-year-old boy who had come to treatment because of his fears of flying. In order to fight against this fear he had started training to be a pilot and at first this seemed to work and he could do it without problem. However, this defence soon broke down and he looked for professional psychiatric help. He spoke about the panic that invaded him whenever the plane went through a zone of turbulence and he imagined that the plane would crash and he would die. It was not difficult to show him how the turbulence he feared most was that of his internal world where he struggled with unresolved sexual and aggressive conflicts for which he felt he deserved to die. The sensation of falling with the plane also contained an unconscious sexual excitement which had been unconsciously repressed and transformed into a painful and frightening situation.

Fears of contamination—which can include irrational fears of being poisoned or infected with HIV—may overlap with obsessive compulsive processes. Such fears may be manifested in excessive hand-washing or avoidance of situations felt to be particularly dangerous. The adolescent suffering from these fears may be partially aware of their irrationality and so attempt to cover them with a cloak of rationalisations. These symptoms will usually have been evident in latency, and represent a resurgence of earlier unresolved conflicts. They can be understood along the lines of phobias and hypochondriacal fears. External cultural factors might be used unconsciously by the adolescent to rationalise his internal fears and some parents might go along with such rationalisations.

Treatment

The use of anti-depressant medication may be indicated and be very useful in an acute depressive state, when the young person may be too withdrawn emotionally to engage in psychological treatment; anxiolytic medication may also be useful in reducing high levels of anxiety affecting the young person's ability to function. However, in general, some form of psychological treatment will be necessary if the adolescent shows prolonged depressive and anxiety symptoms. This may range from cognitive behavioural therapy, family or group therapy, to intensive psychoanalytic therapy.

A thorough assessment, probably carried out over several appointments, is essential in identifying the underlying nature of the symptoms and in deciding what may be the most appropriate form of treatment. The assessment itself can be very helpful in beginning the process of engaging the young person in thinking about his difficulties. An important part of the assessment will need to be concerned with establishing the degree of risk of suicide in the depressed adolescent. Again, engaging the young person in trying to understand his behaviour and symptoms is central.

Many adolescents are ambivalent about seeking help from professionals who are regarded as authority figures and therefore representatives of the parents, with whom they are struggling explicitly or at a deeper emotional level. It is important for the professionals to be aware of this in their provision of treatment; the adolescent may need to leave treatment on more than one occasion before feeling safe enough to continue in a consistent manner.

Adolescents suffering from mild to moderate depression may only need short-term treatment, but those suffering from prolonged depression which has severely affected their ability to function, are likely to require fairly long-term treatment. Similarly with anxiety and phobic symptoms, short-term therapy may be sufficient; however if these symptoms are part of a depressive illness longer-term therapy will be needed.

The involvement of parents when the adolescent is being seen individually can be a very sensitive issue, particularly when working with the older adolescent; unless the young person is unable to give consent, this should always be discussed openly with him, otherwise it is likely to provoke the adolescent to leave treatment. Parents may need to be involved where there is a suicide risk, when the adolescent is unable to properly care for himself, or when there is a significant degree of family involvement in the adolescent's difficulties.

CHAPTER THREE

Academic failure

A cademic failure and, to a lesser extent, lack of enthu-
siasm vis-à-vis their children's studies, is one of the
great parental preoccupations during most of the
period of adolescence. What to advise parents in such situations is always a difficult and delicate matter. It is, of course,
their duty to encourage their children to study but it is also our
duty to make parents aware of a few facts.

Is adolescence the ideal period of life to learn and to apply
oneself to formal academic studies? We do not think so. In order
to understand why, we need to remember what happens during the first five years of life, what happens to these children
as they gradually progress through the main developmental
phases: oral, anal, urethral, and phallic. Not only do we need
to think about what happens to children but also what happens to their relationships with those around them: parents,
siblings, nannies, and other important relatives such as grandparents, uncles, aunts, etc. As has been already described by
our colleagues in the precedent volumes in this collection, this
is not an easy period, and its culmination is certainly difficult—
the Oedipus complex and its resolution are the equivalent of
a most tempestuous love affair, one that is bound to have an

unhappy end. Afterwards, things change drastically and, after the storm, calm arrives. What follows is known as the latency period and it is the one during which the child is more receptive to teaching and the period during which he is more keen and ready to learn. Most of his psychic energy has been withdrawn from the previous "childish" areas of interest and he is now invested in learning about everything in his new, ever-wider world. At this stage, children become difficult prospective psychoanalytic patients, as they do not wish to look back, but they are, by the same token, ideal students, as their thirst for knowledge intensifies. Adolescence is exactly the opposite of latency! Nothing could be more different, and we shall now try to remind ourselves, *grosso modo*, of the main aspects of the adolescent period.

If we remember that during adolescence there is a reawakening of the conflicts and problems of the first five years of life and of those belonging to the Oedipus period, we shall begin to understand why academic achievement is a very difficult task. We shall try here to describe some of the problems, in the hope of helping worried parents to accompany their adolescent children through this difficult journey.

Let us begin by reminding ourselves that adolescent reactions belong at an intermediary point on the line of development between mental health and mental illness and that while people cross the border many times during their lives, adolescents do it all the time. This is as difficult for parents as it is for adolescents. Mental health depends on workable compromises, and on the resulting balance of forces: between parents and children, but mostly between the different components and demands of the diverse aspects of the adolescent personality. This balance is fragile and likely to be altered by any changes in internal or external circumstances, namely changes in the adolescent himself or in his environment, which includes his family. For each step forwards there is an accompanying step backwards as every change in any part of mental life disturbs the equilibrium previously gained and therefore new adaptive measures have to be taken.

During adolescence those changes may affect what we call the instinctual drives, namely the sexual and aggressive impulses to which the adolescent is now submitted under the influence of his new body—a body now capable of doing the things that, as a child, he wanted to do but was not always able to. The adolescent is in the position of the dreamer to whom are suddenly bestowed the special powers to *realise* his dreams. It is, needless to say, a frightening, albeit attractive, proposition.

In order to establish some sort of order and equilibrium, the psychological agency we call the ego, and whose task is to manage and control forbidden wishes, has to be taken into account. The temptation is to put into action all sorts of early infantile sexual and aggressive acts, plus the subsequent unconscious incestuous fantasies that may still be active towards the end of adolescence: these are the main cause of changes in the ego and are as characteristic of adolescent turmoil as is unpredictability. The agency we call the ego makes serious attempts to keep all that has been described above under control through an increase of the use of defences that bring into play further repressions. The adolescent may now be inclined to neutralise certain impulses by turning them into their opposites: for instance, his inclination to be dirtier and untidier than ever might be replaced by rituals and an obsession with cleanliness and tidiness. He may become prone to blame others for his own desires, may rationalise them, and, more rarely, may transform his unacceptable wishes into something socially acceptable: for instance, transforming his inclination to be destructive and aggressive into an interest in physical activities such as the gym, martial arts, or even the army. This means that the increased activity aimed at controlling the impulses alternates with eruptions of uncontrolled impulses; this is the unpredictable adolescent—we never know which aspect we are going to find. To complicate things further we have to remind ourselves that these changes also affect relationships with people in the external world whom the adolescent loves. The presence and influence of those he loves continue to have a very disturbing effect on the adolescent and he has to fight them with all his might. He behaves as if he believed that nothing helps better than discarding the people he loves, particularly his parents and especially the parent of the opposite sex. Everything which helps to create a distance from his parents is well received by the adolescent, be it a choice of career, partner, friends, or even sexual preference. The adolescent believes, during this phase, that the only way to deal with the disturbing effect that the presence of his parents has on him is to write them off, which is, understandably, a great source of worry for them. Parents need help and guidance in understanding this aspect of the older adolescent's behaviour so that they can continue their struggle to maintain contact with him in spite of his apparent rejection. Some adolescents replace their parents with another admired, but less incestuously dangerous, adult such as a teacher, a film or pop star, a sporting hero, etc. The influence of teachers at this stage is very important, particularly regarding academic failure, as shown in popular films such as *The Prime of Miss Jean Brodie* (based on the book of the same name by Muriel Spark), *Dead Poets Society*, etc. If the young person falls under the spell of a charismatic teacher who knows how to guide his young pupil, academic failure may be less of a threat. This is not always the case and the adolescent may instead turn to his peer group where a member may be chosen as the unquestioned leader whose moral and aesthetic values are blindly followed. Following a delinquent leader, or one who lives in a world of drugs and alcohol, represents a risk we do not need to explain as the dangers of such activities are addressed in other chapters of this book. The same applies to leaders whose equivocal religious or political beliefs the adolescent may end up uncritically adhering to.

The importance of sexual problems in adolescence should not make us forget the significance of the role of aggression, which nowadays seems to have become even greater and the repercussions of which cause justifiable concern not only to parents but also to teachers and to society in general.

To all this we must add the feelings of loss and sadness which accompany adolescents as they lose the privileges of childhood and enter the demanding world of adults with its imposed social and financial responsibilities and duties.

We definitely do not mean that adults should give in to adolescents because of the turmoil they are going through. Even the older adolescents about whom we are writing, still need parental authority, though this should not be imposed by force but through reasonable compromise. It is in order to help parents reach such reasonable compromise that we feel a better knowledge, or perhaps a reminder, of what it is to be an adolescent is an asset, rather than an excuse to allow their children to do as they please.

It is therefore unfortunate that the period of adolescent commotion and turmoil should coincide with the time when many academic demands are being placed on young people, who are expected to achieve what are, at times, almost impossible goals in school and university and when choosing a career or a profession. We are all aware of the many failures in this respect and also of the tragic consequences which at times follow such failures. We must remind parents that these are not necessarily due to their children's unwillingness, laziness, or incapacity, but to the great demands on the young person at a time in his life when all his energies are centred around finding a solution to all the major problems mentioned above, which are part of normal growth and development. An adolescent who is a model of virtue and an exemplary student, could be an adolescent who is failing to deal with some of the problems appropriate to his age: he has retreated into his studies in an attempt to keep his conflicts, sexual and aggressive, at bay, similar to the frightened young child who hides under his blanket at night to protect himself from the nocturnal monsters he fears being attacked by. While we understand why such an adolescent may be the dream-child of many parents and a delight to them, it is not necessarily going to help his well being or his progress towards the next developmental step: young adulthood, the stage when the person reassembles himself once again and, learning from his past, readdresses his psychic energies to fulfil the dreams that, until now, he has been unable to achieve. Such dreams, by the way, may not be very different from those dreams and ambitions his parents had for him, but the timing—towards the end of the adolescent period—for them to coincide was simply wrong. Parents may then realise that waiting and struggling to maintain close contact with their adolescent children has paid off.

It has been our intention here to help parents to understand why their children may have difficulties in applying themselves to academic tasks while simultaneously having to deal with numerous other problems typical of that developmental phase. The message we wish to convey is that, while it is true that, towards the end of adolescence, the young person has to be invested in learning and has to begin to prepare himself for the future in terms of profession or occupation, it is not the end of the world if his marks are not always brilliant and if his zeal and strengths are not always aimed at his studies. Many youngsters who have been mediocre students later move on to make adaptive choices which not only help them personally but may also help them to become outstanding in whatever field they end up choosing to work in, be it in the sciences or the arts or in business. It is important for parents to realise that by disapproving too severely of their children's apparent lack of interest in their studies, and through insisting that their children must be top of the class, they may be reinforcing the need that young people (particularly rebellious older ones) have to oppose their parents.

CHAPTER FOUR

Aggression

A ggression is part of human development from the beginning of life and as such we can talk about it as an instinct. Aggressive tendencies of all sorts constitute a considerable proportion of human behaviours, of human drives. These tendencies are necessary for us to go forward in life, to achieve, to survive. In this sense we can talk of the energy that constitutes normal and constructive aggression. Aggressiveness may also be a reaction to frustration and be aimed at overcoming such frustrations. Defensive aggression is a normal response to another form of aggression, namely violence or external attack, whilst pathological aggression is aimed at destroying others or oneself and is the main essence of unjustified violence. In adolescence aggression acquires a particular character and function which, by its urgent presence, causes confusion and concern among young people or to the adults around them. At this point of adolescence the character of aggression changes, as now the young person has a body that allows him to carry out damaging and destructive acts of aggression which can no longer be easily controlled by adults.

Aggression in adolescence also reflects the developmental necessity for the adolescent to define himself as a separate person and is thus part of the developmental push forward from childhood to adulthood. As with any developmental move forward there is a great deal of anxiety evoked within the individual which, at times, is easily communicated to adults in a veiled plea for help.

The adolescent needs to be able to use healthy aggression in order to succeed at school, at work, socially, and in the world in general. This becomes more and more important towards the end of adolescence in order to facilitate the completion of multiple tasks. Healthy aggression may become pathological and used for defensive purposes, thereby becoming less available for growth and more clearly a sign of disturbance. In late adolescence we would expect to see a decrease in the earlier forms of destructive aggression and an increase in more constructive aggression.

Aggression can become a source of pathology in adolescence. The main causes for pathological aggression may be:

- The resurgence of infantile traumas caused by abuse, neglect, deprivation, both real fresh ones (not infantile) and also memories triggered off by new experiences.
- Fears of regression to childhood dependence associated with incestuous anxieties. We are referring here to aggression as a defence against heterosexual anxieties caused by the disturbed and disturbing resurgence of unconscious incestuous desires and also by the old, conscious and unconscious, fear of the *vagina dentata*. By this we refer to the well known fear experienced by boys that their penises will be trapped inside the vagina and perhaps cut off. This fear is often disguised, albeit thinly, in stories and jokes about lovers unable to separate physically after sexual intercourse, animals (usually dogs) in the same situation, etc.

- Confusion about sexual identity. Adolescents who may experience uncomfortable unconscious transitory homosexual feelings towards peers often deal with them through aggression and violence. This happens both in girls and boys but more often among boys. It is an important aspect of bullying. It is enough for a furtive look from another boy in the street or in the underground to unleash a vicious attack from an insecure boy whose sexual identity feels immediately threatened by that look, irrespective of whether the suspicion is justified or not. This is not very different from the adolescent who has to use violence to defend himself from intense passive, not necessarily sexual, infantile wishes.

- Uncertainty about identity and self-coherence that evokes intense anxiety which is defended against through aggression. (see Chapter Two, on anxiety and depression, which are ubiquitous in adolescence.)

- Adolescents also may be violent in order to fight suicidal feelings caused by intense discomfort in relation to their bodies and what they represent, especially if they see their bodies as the source of homosexual, dirty, crazy desires. If the adolescent succeeds in projecting all this onto others, he will attack in them the hated part of himself, but if that fails, the risk of turning the violence against himself in a suicidal manner becomes more extreme.

The adolescent is by definition "paranoid". We mean by this that the adolescent is normally very self-preoccupied and self-centred, even at the late stages of adolescence. On the other hand, the adolescent's need to sort out who he is and to differentiate himself from others—particularly the parents—leads to the use of the primitive defence mechanism called projection, namely the attribution onto others of unwanted aspects of the self. This is important to bear in mind when trying to understand apparently unprovoked attacks and other acts of violence perpetrated by adolescents unable to recognise and contain their own aggressive impulses. These adolescents externalise their aggression and thus imagine that others are attacking, or about to attack, them and it is to this imaginary attack that they react with the apparently unmotivated and unprovoked attack they perpetrate upon others (see Chapter Six, on severe mental illness).

We shall begin by examining aggression at home, which ranges from "normal" bad moods and refusal to tidy the bedroom to more aggressive defiance including both verbal and physical aggression towards parents and siblings. The bad moods and refusal to tidy up may reflect a depressive withdrawal and, at the same time, an attempt to be independent which is hindered by a regression to the toilet training developmental phase (which is about the establishment of control of the self and body boundaries). This is a phenomenon that parents may find very difficult to understand and deal with, especially with their older children who are expected to have reached a higher level of "civilised" behaviour. However, for the adolescent his room represents his private personal space within which he is trying to work out his sense of individuality; it is important for parents to respect this whilst at the same time maintaining their authority in the rest of the house.

Defiant behaviour also reflects the adolescent's struggle with establishing his independence and his conflicting wishes for limit setting from parents, as in the case of the adolescent who insists on being allowed to return home at 5 a.m. but who is also unconsciously asking the parent not to give in to that request. How this is handled by the parent is very important; the adult has to find a reasonable compromise that involves a mixture of respect for the adolescent and at the same time responds to the adolescent's need for the adult's assertion of his authority.

Fights with the parents may be verbal or physical. Whilst verbal aggression is part of normal adolescent behaviour, physical aggression is always a sign of disturbance. In verbal aggression the adolescent shows his capacity to contain aggressive impulses and wishes in words and thoughts, whilst the adolescent who physically attacks a parent has drastically crossed a boundary between thought and action. This very often arises from overwhelming incestuous fantasies and anxieties which the adolescent cannot contain and which he defends against through aggression where physical touch is achieved (the wish gratified) and, presumably, met with punishment (the feared wish is punished). Parents need to find the right balance between the need for their authority to be clearly established and the common sense required to avoid situations that contribute to constant arguments in the house. Some parents, unconsciously, provoke their children into such physical attacks and therefore need professional help to be made aware of their contribution to that kind of situation.

Self-destructive aggression can be expressed in several ways: an undisguised attack against oneself as in the case of suicide; self-mutilation, self-cutting; involvement with "the wrong crowd"; or in disguised form, as in the case of eating disorders, alcoholism, and drug addiction, and different forms of risk-taking behaviour, such as careless driving. We also need to include here other forms of aggression turned against the self such as the current fashion for piercings and tattoos, which are variations of self-mutilation.

Eating disorders, such as anorexia nervosa, bulimia, and obesity, are an increasing source of worry in modern society. However adolescents with these problems are not always recognised and treated appropriately, partly because the adolescent strives to hide his difficulties but also because there are social and cultural factors which contribute to the belittling/ disguise of the severity of these problems. It is not always easy to distinguish when these problems are the result of aggression unconsciously turned against oneself or against the family, especially the parents, or when they are due to the adolescent obsession with image which, if excessive, may reflect problems of self esteem. These problems may not be completely different from those seen in drug addiction and alcoholism, although they are far from identical (see Chapter Five on drug addiction and alcoholism). Eating disorders—which nearly always contain an element of an early disturbance in the mother-child relationship—are worrying when they persist into the final stages of adolescence, and often require professional psychoanalytic, medical, and psychiatric help. They are nearly always the symptom of serious underlying disturbance which cannot and should not be ignored.

The increase in occurrences of violence on the streets links with the developmental need of some vulnerable younger male adolescents to carry a knife in order to ward off castration anxiety and the castrating father. The possession of a knife represents the idealised penis/phallus with which the adolescent boy stands up to the menacing father. While this has always been part of the conscious or unconscious fantasies normally found in young adolescent boys, it has, until recently, rarely been acted out. We wonder about its role in the increase of street stabbings. We need to think about the homosexual component of this, as well, because many boys who stab other boys react, as we have described above, to what they call a "dirty look" from their victim. We need to think about what happens in the internal world of the older adolescents who carry out these attacks. There are two sources of anxiety: one is the displacement of the menacing father onto other youths or adult men; the other is the projection of the boys' own anxieties and fears of the hated part of the self (weakness, disability, difference). By projection we mean the psychological process by which the young person disowns a hated aspect of himself and subsequently attributes it to another young person who, in reality, has something in common with that hated quality. When this young person is attacked the perpetrator is not only attacking the victim but also trying to destroy the hated part of himself. This process is usually repeated because the attack, in itself, does not remove the internal problem of the perpetrator who feels unconsciously compelled to find other victims in a vain attempt to solve, externally, a conflict which occurs within himself.

The stabbings usually take place within group or gang fights. In attempting to understand how these clashes occur, the importance of group processes in facilitating this kind of projective mechanisms has to be borne in mind. The role of group and gang culture in adolescence needs to be described: the group is important for adolescents as a setting in which various kinds of identificatory processes take place: the working out of values internal and external, what is regarded as good or bad, developing sources of self-esteem. The group also provides a setting in which the adolescent has to prove himself in order to be reassured externally, to compensate for the absence of internal reassurances of value and worth. The youngsters involved in street fighting often do not possess the ability to articulate their conflicts and, thus, are unable to find a non-aggressive solution to their problems. Bullying, in its various manifestations—as an individual but more often as a group activity—has to be borne in mind when talking about this type of aggression. It is important to understand aggression in groups because individuals in them behave quite differently from the way they would act independently. Inhibitions are lifted and impulses are satisfied and acted out without conflict, and self-esteem is intensified at the expense of others, the victims of bullying; the censoring agency called superego is put into abeyance and, in all this, the power of a compelling idea dominates and determines group behaviour. This is very important in understanding mob violence and other social forms of group oppression; and when the objects of a group's wrath are chosen because they are at a disadvantage it may legitimately be considered as bullying. It seems that the essential feature of bullying is the conviction that it is precisely because a man has fallen from grace that it is legitimate to hit him. (Basini, the victimised boy in

Robert Musil's *The Confusions of Young Törless* is an appropriate example to quote in this respect.)

The participation of girls in street violence is on the increase. They seem to be spectators, vicarious voyeurs, using their mobile phones to film vicious, violent, and, at times, murderous attacks. These not only involve boys but also adults, and are, sometimes, sexual attacks on other girls. Often having witnessed violence at home, these girls are usually, but not always, under the effects of drugs and alcohol, and further research is needed into this relatively recent phenomenon in relation to older adolescents. In the late stages of adolescence we would expect the importance of groups to have diminished and yet the reality is that group violence is on the increase.

Dealing with aggression, both at home and outside, presents parents with difficulties. Physical punishment of the adolescent, especially the older adolescent, is, of course, not ideal, as it just repeats the same violent attack perpetrated by the youth on others; but doing nothing is not helpful either. Young people are very sensitive about feeling patronised or controlled and this needs to be taken into account. Words may not be helpful with youngsters who, for one reason or another, cannot actually hear them or use them. This may happen more often than we like to admit and perhaps parents and teachers need to make an effort to devise other stratagems: what is needed is an educational process whose aims are to enable the young person to express his aggression in a non-dangerous way and to develop greater awareness of it, its roots, and the consequences of its expression.

We should not underestimate the power that some physical, non-intellectual activities—dance, drama, sport, for example—have to help young people in developing self-esteem as well as providing an outlet for aggression. Dance as an activity to help violent teenagers and young adults is a curious activity that seems to have encountered great success in recent years, both in Great Britain and abroad, as several films and documentaries testify. One well publicised example is that of a prison on the island of Cebu in the Philippines where it has been made a compulsory activity for their 1600 inmates after the rather surprised prison authorities became aware of the beneficial effects of dancing. Very noticeable among these beneficial effects was an increase in self esteem and a decrease of violence among the inmates.

Parents, teachers, and all adults in charge of young people need to be encouraged to seek guidance from psychologically informed professionals such as psychoanalysts and other psychotherapists.

The problems underlying severe expressions of aggression against others and against the self require careful professional evaluation in order to ascertain the appropriate treatment. If, in theory, psychoanalysis five times a week may seem to be the ideal solution, this may not always be practical, and the person conducting the treatment has to be sufficiently flexible to adapt to the needs and wishes of a patient who may not be prepared, or able, to accept what is being offered. Here, we think, it is of the utmost importance to concentrate first on making a relationship with the young person with whom, later, a joint, rather than an imposed, choice will be made. Youngsters who are initially hostile and who have come to see us reluctantly, have often been persuaded, through the use of patience and tact, to engage in psychoanalytic treatment and establish a reasonable therapeutic alliance. The use of words, we must remind ourselves as therapists, is a double-edged sword: some adolescents, even at this later developmental stage, may not understand them as symbols but take them literally, hence the need for the therapist to be careful with what he says to these patients. It is important for us to make it clear to the adolescent that we want to know his view on things and help him to come to his own conclusions.

In-patient admission may be required in the case of violent youngsters as well as in the case of those suffering from life-threatening eating disorders. Rather than abandoning them to psychiatric care, we should try to complement it with psychotherapeutic help aimed at enabling the adolescent to understand himself and his actions.

Out-patient treatment is indicated in less severe cases, and both individual and group therapies can be useful, though, we repeat, these adolescents may often find it difficult to engage in traditional forms of treatment, particularly individual treatment. It is in cases like these that we need to consider other alternatives—such as dance and other artistic groups—where the emphasis is not necessarily on the acquisition of insight.

Whatever conclusion we come to in relation to treatment, engaging the parents, even at this relatively late developmental stage, is important in order to ascertain to what extent the personalities of the parents allow them to accept their child's involvement with another adult, that is, the psychoanalyst or psychotherapist. This is not always easy to deal with, as the adolescent will usually ask for his parents to be excluded from the treatment; it is therefore important to explain this to the parents to try to get them to accept guidance from another therapist working jointly with the person seeing their child. This is even more important when it becomes clear, in the course of treatment, that the adolescent's needs are not being met successfully by the individual sessions alone, when the necessity for parental co-operation and guidance becomes obvious.

CHAPTER FIVE

Drug abuse

Problems of substance abuse can occur at any level of society and affect all socio-economic groups. It is the interaction of cultural, environmental, and constitutional elements with the conscious and unconscious forces operating within the individual who becomes an addict (or, in other words, the interaction of his inner and external worlds) that contribute most significantly to the creation of this condition. Whatever the reasons and circumstances surrounding the young person who uses illegal drugs and/or alcohol, parents must be in no doubt as to the seriousness of their children's predicament. Drug and alcohol abuse are an indication of psychological distress in need of remedy.

The adolescent who struggles with emotional conflicts can find himself in the very difficult position of having to make all sorts of readjustments and having to deal with the subsequent new conflicts and anxieties. When things go wrong, adolescents may be unconsciously compelled to develop psychological and/or physical symptoms in their attempt to look after themselves. When the resources of his internal world fail him, the adolescent often seeks solace in external consolations such as drugs, alcohol, sexual acting out, or delinquent behaviour.

Dependency on substances or on pathological conduct becomes the only means of having a sense of belonging; and we then see completed in adolescence an unresolved pathological process that started in childhood, when dependency on those around the child did not offer the necessary feeling of safety. We frequently notice that dependence in the young person is accompanied by a crisis. For the youth, childhood has passed, but adult life in the future cannot always be seen clearly. The greater freedom and opportunities to act upon instinctual drives that adolescence offers are not always accompanied by a satisfactory sense of independence and self-sufficiency nor by a greater tolerance of the dependence on their parents as is the case until adulthood is reached.

Trying to understand the reasons why young people abuse alcohol and/or drugs is not an easy task. A full assessment of such cases will certainly throw a greater light on the subject and it is important to bear in mind the relevance, to the addict, of any changes in self-perception when under the effects of the drug. This leads to the question of what changes they may be trying to achieve. Drugs have different effects on different individuals and it is very difficult to differentiate between psychological and pharmacological effects. There have been important changes in the attitudes to, and the use of, drugs in youth culture over the last three decades. Nowadays the use of recreational drugs at weekends in clubs has become part of youth culture but there is still a significant difference between that and the development of a more serious addiction. Some individuals are more susceptible to becoming addicted than others. Often, young people use drugs for thrills, to obtain sexual gratification, or as a substitute for it, and for them it is the "buzz" that really matters. They may or may not become addicted to the substance they abuse. These substances may be used only occasionally, to produce pleasurable sensations when the lack, or excess, of feelings becomes intolerable to the individual. But we also find other adolescents who take drugs in order to experience the feeling of nirvana in order to ease the despair and misery they experience, as in the case of some heroin users who, under the influence of the drug, no longer care about anything. In the words of an ex-patient: "Heroin is a calming thing. It's the little place you can always turn to and it puts a cloud over everything."

While it is true that some drug users can be thought of as experimental users and controlled users, it should be remembered that adolescence is not characterised as a period of moderation and self control; the younger the adolescent is, the less likely he is to control the use of drugs once he has become involved. The statistical evidence of misuse is greatest among adolescents.

Many youngsters use drugs to increase their self-esteem and in such cases the positive effect on self-esteem outweighs their awareness of the dangers of the drugs.

> **Alan**, a nineteen-year-old heroin addict, the only child of an apparently normal family, good-looking, intelligent, and a good athlete, concealed a violent nature under a pleasant and polite façade. Like many addicts, his self-esteem was low. Previous to his drug-taking, he had a history of outbursts of violence in school, manifested in the bullying of other children and, occasionally, gang fights and vandalism. His eccentricities, shyness, and outbursts of violence had made him a rather isolated youth, with no friends at school. He hated his violence and immediately conveyed to me that heroin made him much more peaceful, more at ease with himself, less aggressive and violent. He felt less paranoid and more willing to make friends with others. He felt better liked, particularly by the trendy youths who were experimenting with soft drugs, cannabis, and even heroin, as something glamorous, attractive, and daring.

For the adolescent who has become an addict, the drug represents an external object endowed with positive and negative characteristics, but however harmful it might be felt to be, it has a necessary function, since the addict feels there is something bad inside him (anxiety, violence, depression, guilt, perversion, psychosis, etc.), and uses the drug as if it were a medicine, to anaesthetise or destroy the badness, to "cure" himself. Drug abusers are "self-medicators", who desperately and vainly try to deal with powerful, intense, and disturbing inner experiences which threaten to overwhelm them. However, it is the addict himself who is in danger of being destroyed.

Considering those youngsters who occasionally abuse drugs and/or alcohol and those who become addicted to them, we must remember that they are not the same. They are a varied and complex group, where the underlying problems range from mild to extremely severe. There is an unfortunate tendency to see these patients as belonging to the same category and many erroneous generalisations result from this misconception. One of these, for instance, is classifying the juvenile delinquent and the addict as one and the same. While it is true that addicts have their fair share of trouble with the law and become involved in delinquent and criminal acts (in the way that children lie and steal in order to obtain their supplies of sweets), they are not to be confused with the psychopath who experiences no internal conflict and cannot create one. Instead he establishes a conflict with the outside world and in so doing uses methods which alter the environment. The young drug abuser, as well as the addict, experiences an internal conflict and tries to resolve it by measures whose aims are to alter the self through the ingestion of drugs and/or alcohol. This difference is an important one and has to be taken into account for the proper understanding and management of these two different conditions, which I will illustrate with the following vignettes:

> **John,** a fifteen-year-old youth, the son of divorced parents, had felt abandoned and rejected by his father whom he had not seen since the age of ten. Undermined by his

mother—who constantly criticised him and who found it difficult to tolerate his presence because it reminded her of her ex-husband—John had very poor self-esteem and had failed disastrously in his studies, despite being of superior intelligence. At school he started mixing with the "bad crowd" and began experimenting with drugs, first with hashish and afterwards with amphetamines, to which he became addicted, after experiencing, for the first time in his life, positive feelings of self-esteem. He felt that "speed" gave him a stronger, more powerful, personality which, he thought, helped him to obtain the admiration of his friends. In the course of treatment he was able to acknowledge his "feelings of inferiority" and how he took drugs in order to "improve himself" and feel "more normal".

Linda, a nineteen-year-old girl with a long history of antisocial activities, which included shoplifting, handling stolen goods, and vandalism, found herself a patient in an adolescent unit as a result of a probation order. She experienced no remorse over her delinquent activities and was convinced she had been caught only as a result of not being "clever enough". The family history revealed an early life of emotional deprivation and a sadomaso-chistic relationship with a mother who had never helped her to master her world, leaving her with the conviction that she could only conquer the environment by altering it if she had "special powers". Magical thinking perme-ated her mental life and she only responded to treatment whenever she felt she was in the presence of a more pow-erful and clever therapist whose "magic" she could steal. She attended an adolescent unit as an out-patient and, in addition to individual psychotherapy, she attended fam-ily therapy meetings which were very helpful to her and her family. She eventually found a partner, had children, and trained, successfully, as a probation officer.

The affect of the addict is usually a troubled and depressed one. There is none of the defiance, self-confidence, and open aggressiveness of the psychopath in him, unless, obviously, he is under the influence of drugs or alcohol. When the delinquent uses drugs, he does it to increase his feelings of omnipotence, not to improve an internal and unconscious feeling of something bad inside him.

The type of drug used will influence our understanding of the young drug abuser, since smoking cannabis cannot be equated with injecting heroin. The choice of a specific drug derives from the interaction between its unconscious psychological meaning and the pharmacological effect of the drug on the particular conflicts that have taken place in the adolescent's psychic structure throughout his development. The choice of drug is certainly not as indiscriminate or capricious as it may appear from superficial observation. The anxious youth may use any drug, while the young psychopath will generally take drugs which will accelerate mental processes. On the other hand, the continuous use of opiates may suggest a psychotic or near psychotic disturbance; the drug is used to avoid the intense psychic pain being suffered. In cases of cocaine and amphetamine addiction we have to think of an important depressive element against which the young person is defending himself. Something similar may be said about the persistent use of alcohol, although here it is important to remember the environmental influences that prevail in certain cultures.

The use of different drugs is related to the effect of the drugs themselves and to the problem the adolescent is trying to "cure". It may be extremely difficult—if not impossible—to distinguish between symptoms resulting from pharmacotoxic effects and those caused by the underlying problems. The fears and anxieties that accompany the adolescent's attempts to make sense of the functions of his body and his mind lead to confusion, and the adolescent readily attempts to mitigate this with a "downer". For example, when the adolescent feels that initial sexual experiences have been a failure of some kind, he is easily tempted to get rid of the resulting desolation, despair, and emptiness by means of the instantaneous, though temporary, relief offered by drugs.

At the centre of the adolescent's turmoil are the uncertainties and doubts about his sexual orientation, which he may try to solve through promiscuity or complete withdrawal from any sort of sexual life. When these attempts fail, he may look for other people in similar circumstances in the hope that sharing his problem with others might improve his experience. In such cases, drug abuse comes to be the common link which constitutes the only possible elective and shared experience.

The disturbing effects which may be produced by hallucinogenic substances such as LSD and others, can be very frightening to the young person, who then turns to another drug to dispel the disturbance induced by the first one. As a result, he may find solace in tranquillisers, cannabis, or amphetamines. The escalation to hard drugs results from the adolescent feeling trapped in a situation where he struggles to keep at bay the menace of disintegration.

The role of drugs in adolescence has, from a developmental point of view, many different and interesting implications. Sociological factors, trends, peer group influence, etc., must be taken into account, as well as psychological factors, when assessing the problem, for drug-taking may be part of the normal adolescent's need to experiment, test, or simply rebel against adult values. On its own this would be, of course, a very simplistic explanation. The use of drugs in adolescence is closely connected with failed attempts to deal with intense aggressive and sexual feelings as well as with the depression we often find in adolescence, which is connected to feelings about losing the privileges of childhood and to the fear of entering adulthood.

The adolescent in trouble with drugs is very much in need of help. Parental collaboration and the right choice of treatment are essential. This is not easy. It is a fact that the number of confirmed addicts asking for treatment is small. The nature of their disturbance predisposes them not to co-operate with the timescale that most psychological treatments demand. The number of analysts and psychotherapists who will accept them for treatment, and, indeed, are able to work with them, is small, and the number of addicts who complete their treatment is even smaller. As in many other areas concerning adolescents, there is no consensus on the treatment and management of these patients. We need to think carefully about what sort of help to offer the adolescent and his parents and this may involve a long, delicate, and difficult period of assessment. Careful consideration of the young person's individual and family problems must be accompanied by an even more meticulous evaluation of his personal external circumstances and his environment in general, including contact with other agencies, relatives, etc. Special consideration must be given to facts such as the severity, frequency, and nature of the addiction, and whether or not the adolescent has previously succeeded in abandoning it. It would be unrealistic to expect the young addict to have given up drugs completely before starting therapy; if the involvement with drugs is such that to start out-patient treatment in such a state would endanger the treatment itself, we suggest that the young person be admitted to an institution for detoxification, after which severe cases should be referred to a specialised residential unit. Whenever it is decided to start treatment outside the clinic or hospital, we must make sure that the adolescent's living conditions are safe, and we strongly recommend establishing a link and collaboration with those living with the addict. Because the relationship between the adolescent and the therapist is of vital importance, the person treating him must be prepared to take on the parental guiding role without which it is difficult to ensure the survival of the treatment or, indeed, of the patient. Parents and other relatives need an enormous amount of professional guidance and support. Close collaboration with other doctors, probation officers, social workers, hostels, etc. is, in our opinion, a *sine qua non* requirement in these cases.

Individual therapy is one of the several possible treatments, the intensity of which will vary according to the individual's needs and circumstances. Intensive psychoanalytical treatment is the choice for some individuals, although the number of confirmed addicts asking for psychoanalytic treatment is small. Their impatience and intolerance of tension predispose them against the slowness of psychoanalysis. Nevertheless, psychoanalysis offers one of the few hopes of tackling and resolving the problems underlying drug-addiction, but it presents both the adolescent and his family with practical problems that may influence their choice in the direction of other, less intensive, psychological treatments.

If the parents are willing to co-operate, family therapy is, of course, an essential complement to any individual treatment, be it residential or not. In the case of in-patients, this is usually practiced by the individual therapist and another professional. In the case of out-patients, depending on the intensity of the individual treatment (psychoanalysis or some other type of psychodynamic psychotherapy), this may be carried out in similar fashion although with psychoanalytic treatment the psychoanalyst may prefer to delegate the family work to another colleague.

CHAPTER SIX

Severe mental illness

The most common mental illnesses manifesting at this time are schizophrenia, anorexia, and bulimia; schizoaffective disorder may also appear. Drug-induced psychosis and suicidal depression are discussed in other chapters but also need to be borne in mind when thinking about severe mental illness during this important developmental stage at the threshold of adulthood. A thorough psychiatric and psychoanalytically informed assessment is extremely important in order to avoid misdiagnosis and to offer the right treatment to these adolescents and to manage them appropriately: their present and future lives are at great risk.

Late adolescence is a time when symptoms of schizophrenic illness may appear, but one of the difficulties for the psychiatrist is that its symptoms are not the same as in the older adult; this may lead to psychotic symptoms being missed or being over-diagnosed. We do not think a definitive diagnosis should be made at this stage as symptoms may be misleading. It is very important in those cases in which a diagnosis of schizophrenia is being considered, to assess if there are signs of foreclosure of the developmental process of adolescence as well as to examine the state of reality testing; that is, of the adolescent's capacity to distinguish fantasy from reality (or to question the validity of his perceptions of external reality). An adolescent who cannot differentiate reality from fantasy or who is unable to question his perceptions is quite likely to be ill. This state of affairs is very different from the much more fixed character of adult psychotic states: there is an important difference between those states and the distortions due to the developmental process of adolescence. Psychotic, or apparently psychotic, symptoms in adolescents tend to be more fluid, not fixed as they are in adult psychosis; psychotic symptoms may also be induced by drugs (such as amphetamines) in predisposed individuals and such episodes of psychotic illness need to be distinguished from a more chronic illness process. Another important difference is the reversal, during adolescence, of the pathological process, something that does not occur in the case of well established adult psychotic illnesses. Of course, it may well be that by the end of adolescence an ongoing psychotic process has been established, but this is not necessarily always the case and such an outcome might be avoided if the symptoms/condition are noticed early enough and properly treated.

It is uncommon—although not unheard of—for manic-depressive illness to be diagnosed at this time, as this illness usually presents later in adulthood. This is to be differentiated from the common mood disturbances of adolescence. The modern tendency to deal with mood disturbances in adolescence with drugs such as lithium should be approached with caution, as there is no evidence that the depressive illnesses in adolescence, even psychotic depression, are connected with the bipolar disorders which are treated with lithium in adult patients. In psychiatry there is a tendency towards over-simplification in diagnosis. There is also an increasing tendency to overuse anti-depressants in treating adolescents, which may mask symptoms of serious depression and prevent the young person from receiving appropriate psychological help early enough.

Schizophrenic illness may manifest in the following ways: withdrawal, increased anxiety, paranoid behaviour, manic behaviour, violence, problems with the law, drug abuse, academic failure, strange behaviour, aggression, unrestrained promiscuity, particularly in girls, and any marked change in behaviour. Suicide attempts and serious self harm, such as cutting and burning, which represent psychotic attacks on the (new and rejected) sexual body are equally worrying. Compared with younger adolescents, the sexual body should, at this stage, be accepted and integrated into a sense of identity. The adolescent, aware that something is happening to him that he cannot explain, may make great efforts to hide what is wrong, and the diagnosis may not be made for some time. Much depends on the quality and intensity of the symptoms presented by the young person and on the defence mechanisms employed by him, the way in which he copes with the disturbance they represent.

An adolescent with an incipient psychotic illness may present a confusing picture to parents and professionals; this can lead to a series of consultations with a variety of professionals and a fragmentation of care. There may be resistance on the part of parents and professionals to recognise a psychotic illness in an adolescent, alongside the adolescent's own fears and withdrawal. The question of a proper diagnosis, although important, may be unhelpful if the pursuit of a label becomes a preoccupation. It is more important for the professional to inform the parents that there is a serious illness which needs to be addressed. When there are several different professionals involved, it is important for them to communicate with each other and to work together.

It may be difficult to distinguish self-consciousness and ideas of reference, which can be normal in adolescence, from paranoia, but the intensity and quality of the experiences might give a clue to what is going on. It may be normal for an adolescent to feel that people are looking at him in the street, but an ill adolescent is likely to have fixed beliefs about being persecuted in some way—neighbours listening in to his calls or interfering with his post, or a more elaborate set of delusional beliefs about being persecuted because he is a very important person, or that the television is transmitting special messages to him.

Through the use of psychologically informed assessment, we can distinguish a paranoid psychosis which may remain encapsulated, from a schizophrenic illness with negative symptoms interfering with all areas of functioning.

> **Peter** was a twenty-one-year-old young man, very intelligent and likeable, who gradually started showing strange behaviour: one day he said that he knew that his upstairs neighbours listened to everything he was doing in his flat, knew all his moves, and interfered with his mail. He wanted to demonstrate how this was possible, producing a box through which he said I would be able to hear everything he did and said if he went outside of the room. When I explained that I could hear nothing, he continued to believe that the machine worked, thus showing he was out of touch with reality. Peter was a worrying young man whose disturbance required psychiatric intervention. He was completely preoccupied with his concerns and unable to study, work, or lead a normal life. He had no friends and his relationship with his family was seriously impaired.

> **James** was a fifteen-year-old boy who felt compelled to pick up pieces of paper in the street because he believed they contained information about him. Although he could not stop himself from doing this, he knew that his actions were illogical. His sense of reality was intact despite his actions. The messages he looked for were related to his intense anxieties about his sexuality. His difficulties were

helped by psychotherapy where he could speak about
them and obtain help to understand his anxieties.

Simon was a seventeen-year-old public school boy who
was a heroin addict. He attended a drug clinic where
he followed a methadone replacement programme and
eventually gave up heroin. It then became clear that his
addiction was helping him to keep a schizophrenic illness
at bay; he became withdrawn, neglected himself, took to
the streets and became homeless, and eventually had to
be admitted into hospital.

Adolescents with eating disorders, be it anorexia nervosa,
bulimia, or obesity, are the cause of great anxiety for relatives and doctors because of the challenge they present to
those looking after them. Eating disorders have become more
common in recent decades and, despite several theories surrounding their origin, it is not always possible to see clearly
the cause of the problem. Some preoccupation with weight is
normal in teenage girls and, to a lesser extent, in boys, but it
may reach the point when their physical appearance becomes
a cause for concern, and their health is at risk. There is a difference between girls who want to imitate fashion models,
or certain athletes and ballet dancers, who develop eating
disorders motivated by the ideals of beauty and physical
perfection, and youngsters who can no longer see the precari-
ous physical state they have reached. After some degree of
weight loss menstrual periods will cease. When the weight
loss is extreme—for instance below 40 kg—hospitalisation
is required. Other cases may benefit from psychotherapy;
research has indicated that family therapy is more effective in
treating adolescents under fifteen with anorexia, whilst individual psychotherapy is more effective for adolescents over
fifteen. Cognitive behavioural therapy may be a very useful
first treatment for adolescents with bulimia. In all cases early

effective treatment may prevent the development of a chronic illness state. In recent years the number of young men with anorexia and bulimia has increased and the reasons for this are not yet clear.

> **Susan** is a nineteen-year-old girl, an only daughter, who goes through episodes of over-eating to such an extent that her stomach becomes abnormally distended and is at risk of rupture. Behind these binges there is a fantasy of being pregnant; she takes pictures of herself in this distended state. Her disturbance is related to problems in her family relationships, a history of family trauma, and a very disturbed relationship with her mother. She has been in five times a week analysis which has been very helpful in her case and has kept at bay the threat of a psychotic illness. Psychoanalysis has enabled her to find healthier resolutions to her underlying conflicts. Without this treatment she is likely to have remained chronically ill and unable to function independently.

Adolescents of both sexes who become homeless or go into prostitution may be suffering from a psychotic illness. Some adolescents who are homeless may have run away from abusive home situations and may be seriously depressed and in danger of getting pulled into taking drugs, and this may then become a route into prostitution. At this stage all sorts of unusual or perverse sexual practices—that may not have been, developmentally, out of place earlier in younger adolescents where such activities and fantasies can be part of the normal experimentation that takes place—are now at risk of becoming entrenched or fixed character traits in adulthood. They may, on the other hand, be indicative of underlying ongoing psychotic processes that require professional attention and tactful handling both for the young person and for their parents and families.

Suspected psychotic disturbances may require hospital admission and/or psychiatric intervention in order to carry out a full assessment, which may lead to the prescription of medication in order to control the psychotic symptoms and enable the young person to make use of psychological help. It is absolutely essential to engage the parents, and other adults involved with the older adolescent, in the therapeutic situation and to provide parents with support and professional help, especially when the parents' problems have, consciously or, more frequently, unconsciously, contributed to the adolescent's breakdown. It is also important, in cases of hospital treatment, to try to refer the adolescent to an adolescent unit rather than to a general psychiatric ward. Adolescent units specifically cater for the needs of a younger population and their staff has been trained for that purpose.

CHAPTER SEVEN

The therapist's angle

It is rare to find ourselves facing a situation which, in spite of its difficulty, so strongly stimulates the interest and psyche of the professional as happens when we treat adolescents.

This is the sub-specialty which most requires a dynamic understanding of psychic life, a point of special interest to all those who are interested in the subject of mental health. Although it is true that for a deep understanding of our psychic life psychoanalysis seems to be, amongst the various psychiatric approaches, the most ambitious, many of us believe it to be indispensable for working with adolescents of all ages. We wish to draw the attention of those interested in working with young people to some of the difficulties we encounter during this turbulent period in the life of a human being. The difficulties we refer to are not only those of young people but also (or perhaps, even to a greater extent) our own. No other field in psychiatry lends itself, to such an extent, to the acting out of our psychopathology. The adolescent is subjected to so many inner and outer pressures that he can hardly contain them by himself and in himself (as is the case for an adult) or tolerate the restraining steps offered by the world of adults (as is the case with children, for obvious reasons). Projective mechanisms play a very important role in this phase and those of us who are involved in this work are familiar enough with the phenomenon of "infection by the adolescent".

An understanding of the dynamics of adolescence from the point of view of development is a *sine qua non* condition for our task, enabling us to differentiate behavioural traits which are due to transitory problems and are therefore normal, from those which express a deeper psychological disturbance. Or, in other words, taking these factors into account makes diagnostic evaluation easier and assists us in achieving the main therapeutic objective: change and growth. We have referred to the main aspects of adolescence many times in other chapters but, at the risk of repeating ourselves, we would like, at this point, to revisit some of them.

If we could bear in mind more frequently the enormous difficulties which the adolescent (or his parents) has to deal with before deciding to ask for professional help, we would refrain from trying to reassure him that "these are things which usually happen at this age", that the problem will soon be over, to "be a little patient", and other similar expressions: these confirm the adolescent's frequent conviction that adults (just like his parents) either do not understand him or are simply not interested in his personal world. A similar or worse effect is obtained with threats—such as being sent to hospital "if he does not behave" or being sent to a reformatory, or expelled from school—or simply by ignoring him. We wish to emphasise this point because there are many cases which are dealt with lightly and where we might miss the opportunity to prevent serious disorders, the nature of which may only be possible to recognise when it is too late and very little or nothing can be done.

This is an age which is normally characterised by multiple changes in the individual (apart from his physical development) and there is nearly always evidence of inner emotional turmoil, even at the end of adolescence. All this affects and worries parents, teachers, and other adults. This turmoil consists largely of the adolescent's efforts to achieve his independence. The "model", exemplary adolescent who does not show any signs of emotional conflict is probably making an excessive use of repression as a defence mechanism and is failing to find a solution to the problems pertaining to this stage, with the sad consequence of the appearance of unresolved personality disorders in adult life. The repeated contradictions of the adolescent's behaviour are usually the result of his attempts to assert his maturation, but without giving up the advantages of childish dependence, the eternal "to be or not to be" of the adolescent. Sadly, he usually has no insight on how this contradictory behaviour affects those in his world.

Much as in his earlier life, the adolescent experiences conscious and unconscious sexual and aggressive impulses, but he now has a body that is able to put into practice the wishes and fantasies that he was unable to act upon before. This has to be born in mind when trying to understand many of the phenomena presented by our patients and which raise such intense concern in us when we try to help them.

There are not many parents who can witness with serenity the spectacle of the adolescent in the challenging process of becoming independent. Whether we like it or not, these young people always put us in a difficult position. The therapist's function is, certainly, that of an additional parent, but in a more contained, more neutral manner. Before interpreting, intervening, helping, or establishing limits, we have to accept the transference and understand its meaning, endeavour to understand how the adolescent sees us in relation to his world, what role we are playing in it, and how he is integrating us in his reality. This process of understanding stirs up many conscious and unconscious memories of experiences of our own adolescence and it is vital that we endeavour to sort out what belongs to our own life and what is, in fact, part of our adolescent patient's life.

To consider the adolescent as a big child or, on the other hand, as someone on his way to "something" more important (that is, adulthood), is to denigrate the importance of his present life and is a mistake; the consequence is the loss of the purpose of the treatment, which is, mostly, to foster change and development. The difference between children, adolescents, and adults can be understood through the observation of the transference in the three stages (childhood, adolescence, adulthood) and the various ways in which the child, the adolescent, and the adult behave when in psychodynamic therapy. The unconscious incestuous nature of transference (unless the patient is a psychopath or a borderline case) is seen by the patient as unreal and he responds accordingly. In the child, who is still sexually immature, there is as yet no struggle to secure a definite sexual organisation and he still does not, therefore, equate pathology with abnormality, that is, a child usually does not consider his wishes to sleep with his parents as abnormal and, by the same token, the defences against the repetition of equivalent actions in the therapeutic situation are fewer or may not be present.

In the adolescent patient we observe something quite different; the incestuous desires are always present in the transference but he fights against them intensely, partly due to superego prohibition but also because his bodily sexuality, around which the fight against himself is taking place, is now considered to be the cause of his pathology. Pathology and (sexual) abnormality are now synonyms, in the sense that the adolescent's superego, for the first time, disapproves of pathology and therefore of his own, now sexually mature body. Simultaneously, the adolescent (who now feels that his present sexuality is abnormal) demands that the therapist should accept it as normal. Needless to say, our acceptance of this would be equal to succumbing to the adolescent's destructive impulse, which is apparently addressed against the therapist but which is, in fact, unconsciously directed against himself in order to perpetuate the pre-Oedipal relationship with the object of love by means of a regressive mechanism.

Points of reference for the initial diagnostic evaluation

We can consider, *grosso modo*, three periods in the adolescent's development:

From twelve to fourteen years of age

This is when we find that the main worries revolve around adaptation to the first physical changes, and when the young adolescent fights against any sign of loss of control insofar as sex and aggression are concerned. He often struggles with feelings of loneliness, isolation, depression, and the wish to be independent of the parents. We must pay special attention to: a) the adolescent who only relates to other school mates by provoking their aggression, one way or another; b) the lonely adolescent; c) the one who suddenly does very badly at school.

We have to consider premature sexual experiences with every degree of care, above all heterosexual ones, as their meaning at this age is not always clear and frequently reflect deeper problems. Masturbation or homosexual experiences are the adolescent's first efforts to experiment with his body (or with another body similar to his) which has recently acquired its physical and sexual maturity, and should therefore give us less cause for concern. The degree of accompanying anxiety and guilt will give us an indication as to what is worrying the adolescent and what is at the root of these worries, which in the normal adolescent can be due to lack of information, but in the case of a disturbed adolescent will be linked to pathological fantasies.

From fourteen to sixteen

This is the zenith of adolescence and no one has described what happens in this phase better than Anna Freud in The *Ego and the Mechanisms of Defence* (1936) and in *Adolescence* (1958). We do not wish, therefore, to prolong what would be a laboured dissertation and shall only mention some of the most usual defence mechanisms present at this age: 1) defences against affective ties which link them to the first love objects: a) displacement of the libido; b) inversion of affection; c) turning in of the libido towards the self, and d) regression; and 2) defences against impulses (genital and pre-genital): a) asceticism; b) excessive intransigence.

> There is in their aetiology at least one additional element which may be regarded as exclusive to this period and characteristic for it: namely that the danger is felt to be located not only in the id impulses and fantasies but in the very existence of the love objects of the individual's Oedipal and preoedipal past. (Anna Freud, 1958, p. 268.)

We see more clearly in this period the adolescent's efforts to gain emotional independence from his parents and the well known complications that follow these efforts, the near-obsessive preoccupation with his body which explains the narcissism of the typical adolescent, etc. Masturbation in the male is very important as a means of experimenting with his already mature body. Girls are more worried about their looks, femininity, and social relations. Although avoiding the opposite sex points towards the possibility of the existence of problems, promiscuity is a much more serious symptom. Homosexual relationships are not yet necessarily a sign of abnormality but must be taken into account for the future assessment of the adolescent's sexual development.

From sixteen or seventeen to twenty or twenty-one

This is the phase to which this book is dedicated and it is now when signs of pathological or normal development can be more clearly observed. The adolescent experiences this period as a critical one in his life. This is the point in time when his sexual identity begins to define itself: heterosexual relationships are already a part of normal development, but homosexual ones raise the advisability of a detailed investigation of the young-ster's self and object images.

The professional and the adolescent

Perhaps the crucial point of the treatment of these patients lies in the evaluation not only of the effect that we may have on them but also of the effect that the adolescent has on us. A thorough and meticulous study of the confluence and the complex exchanges which take place between the patient and those looking after him is of crucial importance. At an uncon-scious level the professional may relive any unsatisfactorily resolved conflicts of his adolescence and, generally speaking, we can say that there is a reliving of our adolescence, with all the complications that may ensue, when we treat an adolescent patient.

Many of those who have a special interest in the problems which arise at this age will possibly agree with us that intui-tion and a natural talent are not sufficient for the hard work of penetrating the adolescent's world, to respond to his various needs adequately and to gain and retain his trust. All these are indispensable prerequisites for the success of our task. Those professionals who have been in, or who are in, analysis find the insight analysis provides very valuable; its contribution lies not only in its therapeutic and prophylactic possibilities but also in helping us to develop the capacity to maintain our own psychic balance by means of an improved self-knowledge and a greater insight and acceptance of our abilities and limi-tations. It is unnecessary to say that the ideal solution is not always within our reach (because of such restrictions as time and money) but in its absence there are other alternatives we can turn to: a careful selection (preferably by a therapist with experience in this field) of the staff working in adolescent units;

individual supervision; seminars and lectures of a didactic nature; discussions with colleagues which include the healthy exchange of ideas which is so necessary in our profession; sensitivity groups; clinical sessions; etc.

Contact with the labile psychic structure of the adolescent, bombarded as it is by anxiety and emotionally egocentric, submits our psychic integrity to the hardest and most exhaustive tests. The adolescent's psychic dynamic is very similar to that of the adult's narcissistic and borderline states (with the difference that the adolescent's prognosis is more favourable) and those who have treated this kind of patient know how exhausting and difficult the therapist's task can be and how the use of tact is indispensable.

We do not wish to appear pessimistic but do want to insist on the need to proceed with care when selecting the most appropriate approach in each case. Those of us who work in this field know very well that the treatment of these patients is not only very stimulating but that it also provides us with satisfactions which we do not usually encounter when working with adult patients.

A deep understanding of our counter-transference becomes essential, as the adolescent's emotional attitude towards the therapist is, as we have mentioned earlier, not only a repetition of the past but real, situated in the present and we must therefore be sensitive to it and understand how the patient really sees us, instead of simply assuming that we are seen as just representing people from the past. This test is not always easy to face. There are countless occasions on which we may feel threatened, when all kinds of defensive mechanisms come into action which might make us act out our own or our patients' problems. The personal analytical experience facilitates the "differential diagnosis" between the anxiety caused by disturbances of our emotional economy and that caused by the unconscious perception of the potential danger contained by some of the patient's circumstances. We would like to mention the following vignette:

A therapist received a letter from a young patient who, after having spent some time in a specialist adolescent addiction unit, decided to return to his native town. He telephoned now and then, he even came to London to visit, and everything seemed to be relatively all right. His letter seemed to be a confirmation of all this and yet it did not give the therapist the satisfaction that one usually feels when we see our patients' improvement; instead the therapist was gradually invaded by a feeling of worry and sadness. Two days later, when he was going to reply to the letter, he received a telephone call from his patient's father who informed him that that day his son had "accidentally" died of an overdose.

As the adolescent shows resistance to the therapeutic process more openly than the adult, it is particularly difficult for those of us who come from the field of medicine to control our eagerness to "cure" the patient and to accept that in some cases the possible benefits of our intervention are very limited. An example of the frustration that an analyst can experience in these cases is the unnecessary and indiscriminate use of treatments which we consider inappropriate for adolescents and, in some instances, totally contra-indicated, such as electroshocks, insulin shocks, psycho-surgery, medication, etc. The following story comes to mind:

An adolescent girl who had been referred for psychotherapeutic treatment revealed during the initial interview that she was being treated with electroshocks. As her medical history completely ruled out the adequacy of such treatment we decided to postpone the beginning of the treatment until we had spoken to her psychiatrist. The psychiatrist explained, with great joy, the reason for the electroshocks, that is to say, when he knew that the girl was soon to start her psychotherapeutic treatment and in

view of the fact that she was a little depressed, he thought
that he would do us a favour by "getting her ready" with
the "help" of electroconvulsive therapy!

Less dramatic, but no less important, is the paternalism which,
in our society, where conformism plays an important role,
drives the therapist to force upon the adolescent rules of adjustment and success, personal philosophies, and ideals which one
would not really try to impose upon an adult. It is not a matter
of going to the other extreme and pretending to be a person
without any feelings or beliefs, but of finding the appropriate
balance and flexibility which will allow us to respond to the
patient's changing needs instead of trying to fit him into a rigid
and anachronistic mould. This adult's flexibility must however
be backed by firm rules and principles which, despite the adolescent's complaints and protests, provide him with the feeling
that at least *someone* has the necessary calm and clarity needed
to cope with his internal chaos. To face constant provocation,
hostility, and the adolescent's destructive impulses is not an
easy task and requires that those of us who are responsible for
the adolescent should have great strength of character, whatever our profession or our real function: parents, teachers, therapists, nurses, etc. Nothing frightens the adolescent more than
his omnipotence and its victims, those adults who try to adopt
the short-lived values of the adolescent in their custody. As the
adolescent uses the adult (consciously and unconsciously) as
a model, special care must be taken about the image that one
shows him; it must never be a fragile and irresponsible one.

The fact that certain aspects of the adolescent's behaviour
can appear acceptable, if not attractive, and incite an exaggerated identification and competition, is true not only for other
adolescents but also for certain adults. For this reason we think
it is necessary to clarify once again that the identification with
these patients is only harmless when it is based on empathy and
when it excludes our acting out. We are specifically thinking

of some young auxiliary nurses and their attitude regarding "harmless" drugs such as cannabis, which may be inoffensive for them, but not so for the adolescent who does not possess the same level of maturity and integration.

We observe the way in which the adolescent stimulates certain aspects of our personality in the secret excitement experienced by the psychiatric worker who unconsciously incites explosions of violence, abuse, and obscenity in the adolescent. One example was a young female nurse who always, "without knowing why", managed to provoke situations in which the boys would invariably end up shouting obscenities at her.

In this same category is the irresponsible and disordered use of personal interpretations by the amateur "wild analyst" whose unconscious motivation is either of an exhibitionistic and omnipotent nature or based on aggressiveness towards the adolescent patient whom he secretly envies. The result is the patient abandoning the treatment (a quick escape caused by the fear brought about by such interpretations) or, even worse, if the patient is a masochist, the establishment of a sadomasochistic relationship between therapist and patient in which both find gratification for their respective psychopathologies.

The case of the psychotherapist who decides to "help" the young adolescent to "accept" his homosexuality before his sexuality is actually defined is not very different. In our experience with adolescents of both sexes, in more than one instance adolescents with problems of a transsexual nature have been evaluated psychiatrically and have been given the go-ahead to take the necessary steps to undergo a surgical sex-change operation. It is very important to remember that adolescence is a phase of development and a full sexual identity is not truly established until the adolescent process comes to its end.

Seduction is the most common weapon in the adolescent's efforts to affect the therapist's professional competence. This is due to the fact that contact with the adolescent is an endless source of gratification of our narcissism. We may feel flattered by the adolescent's expressions or displays of love and affection, not taking into account that this "love" is sometimes a defence against the adolescent's unconscious envious wish to destroy all that the adult has. Gifts are the most obvious example. We do not refer only to concrete gifts but also to more subtle ones, as is the case of certain "improvements" in the course of treatment. The adolescent's attempts to manipulate us represent his attempts to counteract his aggressiveness, to substitute a real therapeutic improvement, or to flatter and expose our vanity. Those who have dealt with delinquents are surely familiar with this kind of behaviour. All this does not mean that the adolescent is unable to feel affection and gratitude to the therapist but it would be naïve on our part to accept these gifts as mere expressions of love without endeavouring to analyse their meaning in the context of the therapeutic relationship, of the history of our patients, of their dreams. However the same professional who, in similar circumstances would proceed very cautiously and with common sense vis-à-vis the adult patient, may easily find himself succumbing to the adolescent.

Especially fascinating for the adult can be the political and intellectual attitudes of the young "revolutionary" who externalises his internal revolution by embracing and leading revolutionary causes of every description, provided, of course, they are movements which, rather than offering a solution to the situation they are fighting against, perpetuate a constant state of "revolution".

If we carefully observe this type of adolescent we will find a discrepancy between his intellectual maturity (which in many instances is of great calibre) and his emotional immaturity. We have to be alert so that we are not blinded by the brilliance of these adolescents, and so find an excuse for their contempt for the need to base those actions which lead to reform on the use of reason. The actions of this type of adolescent are based on an impulsive acting out, which is the suggested alternative proposed by these "dissidents" who have remained stuck, emotionally, at the tantrum stage. In the therapeutic situation, our function is that of therapist and our only interest in these matters therefore lies in exploring their unconscious meaning for the patient. Beyond the importance (social, humanistic, or philosophical) that these problems might have (from those points of view) devoting any other kind of interest to them represents a deviation from the therapeutic attitude and temporarily giving up the search for growth and change, which is the aim of the treatment. During the therapeutic session, our only *raison d'être* is that of analysing the patient. It is the unconscious problems involved in this area which must be explored and which require the systematic and methodical analysis of the patient and of the counter-transference on the part of the therapist.

In the face of difficult situations, the therapist may react by adopting a despotic and tyrannical attitude which blocks the way to any efforts made by the adolescent to grow emotionally. Mistakes of this kind may be observed in the way that many children are brought up in our society, where the family is such an authoritarian institution. As a result we find ourselves with an adolescent who arrives at this stage badly prepared to face his identity crisis which, as a consequence, takes a long time to resolve and this late adolescent period becomes abnormally extended. This is not the only way in which our personal discomfort might be reflected in the arduous task of measuring out the use of that authority which the adolescent so badly needs. Others, mistakenly interpreting psychoanalytic concepts such as those of suppression and of repression take the opposite stance, thereby ignoring the adolescent's absolute need to experiment with extremist solutions, which is all very well as long as the experiment can be contained or expressed through thought, and is not acted in reality. Many adolescents, in order to confine their fantasies and "experiments" to the sphere of their thoughts need the external reinforcement which is provided by those who personify authority. When this control or reinforcement does not exist, it is like giving permission to the adolescent to put into practice such fantasies or experiments (which can, in some instances, be dangerous); the young person, with his confusion and without a clear sense of guidance and control, runs the risk of believing that any fantasy can become reality. It is very important that this should be taken into account in therapeutic communities for delinquent adolescents where the problems of aggression and the difficulties in acquiring self-control are an everyday matter. The need for external controls is understood more clearly if we take into account the fact that during childhood there has not, in these cases, been a satisfactory internalisation of the superego controls over aggressive impulses; and so, when in adolescence they are swamped by their own aggressiveness, they lack the internal controls that would enable them to constructively express their impulses rather than putting them into practice, of acting upon them.

It is very common to hear that it is good for the patient to be able to express his feelings, which is all very well as long as it does not imply that we limit ourselves to witness this sort of "vomit"—communicating without attempting to modify it with the help of our interventions or interpretations. Our aim is to give it back to the patient once we have modified it so that the patient incorporates this message into his psychic structure. The patient feels frustrated and disappointed with the therapist who fails to do so because the message the therapist has received threatens the therapist's psychic balance, thus resorting to the acting out which, at the same time, strengthens that of the patient. This situation must be avoided at all costs with criminal personalities.

Faced with a situation which arouses frustration in the professional, in the patient, or in both, the professional can get depressed or feel guilty or inefficient, without taking into account that this situation could easily be a repetition, within the transference and in a more favourable medium for its ulterior transformation, of what originally brought the patient to his consulting room. The professional's understanding of this facilitates the change of the unconscious into the conscious by the young patient and permits the continuation of a more harmonious therapeutic relationship.

To conclude, we would like to draw attention to the tendency, which sometimes exists, to attribute the adolescent's problems to external factors related to figures representing authority in the patient's real life (parents, teachers, guardians, tutors, etc.), forgetting that the adolescent and his individual psychopathology have contributed, especially in the case of the older adolescent, in great measure to the crisis or disturbance which has brought him before us. By then his problems are his own and must be understood and treated as such. No one will deny that external factors are of great importance but even more important is the manner in which the adolescent reacts to what surrounds him. We must aim to learn and understand how the exchange between family events and the inner difficulties of our patients has evolved over the years.

We are aware that there are many points which require a more elaborate exposition; there are also many which are not included, as the subject is very wide and complex. Our intention in writing this chapter has been mainly to stimulate the interest of those who work with adolescents to study and familiarise themselves with these types of problems, the knowledge and control of which make the task so much easier. This task can, certainly, be as hard and exhausting as it can be rewarding.

CHAPTER EIGHT

The parents' angle

A. H. Brafman

The move from adolescence to adulthood is enormously dependent on the social class and the cultural background of each particular individual. In many cultures marriage is an engagement that characterises adulthood, while in others some religious sects see women as fit for marriage from early adolescence, or arrange marriages for their sons whatever their age. Moving out of the parental home is another landmark that in many cultures represents a change from adolescent dependence to adult self-sufficiency and independence—and yet, it is very common in our present British society for the young adult to continue to live in his parents' home. The capacity to earn a living and become self-sufficient is probably the main factor that leads to an acknowledgement of the individual having reached adulthood. However, for many years, as Erikson (1965) pointed out, university studies represented a "moratorium" that society offered those adolescents who needed some time before taking the plunge into the wider adult world. These examples are quoted in order to illustrate the difference between the individual's experience of himself in the world and how his family, peers, and society in general view his developmental achievements.

The previous chapters in this book have focused on the conscious and unconscious changes in the physical, psychological, and emotional make-up of an adolescent as he struggles to find his way towards adulthood. We would like to supplement this picture with an appraisal of the parents' side of their offspring's move into independent adult life.

Having a child implies a commitment to look after his needs and, ideally, an awareness that the passage of time will demand subtle adaptations to that child's developing abilities to care for himself and his increasing involvement with the world beyond the family unit. It is not difficult to conceptualise this process, but when focusing on a particular family, we may have to consider a number of conflicting hypotheses to explain our findings. Each child's constitutional endowment will influence the manner in which he deals with the continuous input he receives from the family and society in which he lives, but equally important is the capacity of each parent to accept the child's decreasing dependence on him or her. For example, in a broken family, the parent in charge of bringing up the child may find it very difficult to make up for the absence of the other parent when the child's needs go beyond their usual level. In such a family, the child's involvement with peers may bring a sense of relief to the parent—and yet, sometimes the single parent may experience a sense of being abandoned by the child. And this cannot but affect the way in which the child is treated.

Broadly speaking, it is puberty that tends to represent the point at which the intimate, close dependence between child and parents gives way to a multitude of subtle and not-so-subtle conflicts resulting from the child's increasing times spent with peers outside the scope of the family home. The moment conflict arises and the parents criticise the company chosen by the youngster, he protests, predictably, against the parents' possessiveness, while the parents accuse him of hostility and ingratitude. To the outsider it may be impossible to establish who is correct, which attitude is cause and which effect—usually, one has to recognise that both child and parents are entitled to their feelings and claims, since what is involved is a developmental step that affects all of them. It is, therefore, not a question of right and wrong; in an ideal situation each participant would grasp, and concentrate on, his own contribution to the conflict—a more productive posture than trying to blame each other.

Once adolescence is in progress, parents have to accept that their child's horizons will widen continuously. Both physical and psychological endowments lead youngsters to explore the world in which they live. From early childhood it may be difficult to establish whether a particular feature of the child's personality and behaviour originates from his constitutional endowment or whether, instead, it is related to his exposure to his environment; when puberty arrives and adolescent development begins, it becomes even more difficult to decide what in the youngster's personality reflects his nature and what results from nurture. When all goes well, this has mere academic importance, but if a problem arises the situation becomes quite complex. It is then very important to try and determine which of the characteristics of the youngster's personality originate from his exposure to the environment in which he was brought up, since this may enable us to evaluate more precisely the potential for change should the youngster move into some specific educational or therapeutic enterprise.

If a child has been brought up in a family with rigid principles, where he has no real scope to choose and develop his personal style, there is a strong possibility that he will grow up adopting and practising the family ethos throughout his adolescence. Occasionally, some of these youngsters will rebel and what happens will depend on the willingness of the parents to tolerate this departure from their principles. If the family reacts by cutting him off from its support, the adolescent may find himself isolated and thrown into a whirlpool of strong feelings, ranging from anger and resentment to guilt, shame, and fear. His sense of abandonment may lead him to seek an alternative source of support and quite often this leads him to contact individuals or groups that he would normally keep away from. Indeed, his rebellion against parental values may follow on from his involvement with these "bad" peers, but if parents are able to help him discuss and analyse his feelings and impulses rather than write him off, the course of events may be very different.

What about a child growing up with parents who are not determined to shape his personality into the prevailing family mould? Perhaps there have always been families like this, but in the recent past, such an "easy-going" attitude has become associated with notions of respect for individual freedom and the right of the child to self-assertion and to the development of his own inborn personality. This formulation has, somehow, a strong appeal to many people, including professionals. However, it contains flaws and mistaken interpretations that should be recognised.

What language will the child speak if not the one used by his parents? Will the child be allowed to grab his food and eat it with his hands, whatever his age? What about the manner in which the child addresses older members of his family? Will mealtimes and bedtime be entirely left for the child to decide? Toilet training is perhaps the best example to discuss this question: indeed there are parents who believe the child should be allowed to "find his own rhythm", but who eventually object to the child urinating and defecating in his trousers.

If we focus on children's abilities and needs, we must recognise that every "normal" child has the potential to adapt his physical endowment to the mores of the family and society in which he is growing up. This is what we call teaching, disciplining, nurturing. But "disciplining" has become confused with "domination" and abuse, which are the very opposites of what is supposed to be respect for the child's individuality.

At the end of the day, we have children who somehow manage to develop their own physical and social rhythm of living, but we find others who feel confused and eventually discover that their habits clash with the attitudes of peers and adults in their world.

It must be appreciated that while these aspects can easily be found in young children, it is impossible to predict how the confused child will develop and reach adolescence and adulthood. But when focusing on an individual late adolescent or young adult, it can be very tempting to attribute some features of his general behaviour, sentiments, and words to an early life where his parents failed to give him an adequate set of rules that would have enabled him to blend with others in society. An example might be the youngster who fails to wash and dress appropriately for his school or job. Is this a sign of rebellion against dominating, demanding parents, or is it, instead, the result of an upbringing where he was allowed to formulate and follow his own rules and wishes?

This question of "easy-going" parents becomes most important when the youngster gets into serious difficulties. The earlier "respect for the child's individuality" can easily lead to an attitude of blaming the adolescent or young adult that is most likely to be felt by the youngster as a rejection and a refusal of help. Perhaps, from the parents' point of view, they are being consistent—as a young person or as an adult, their child is doing no more than displaying and investing in his inborn potentials. This is a regrettable position, since the person in trouble finds himself rejected by those he might have hoped would help him.

During early and mid-adolescence the youngster will usually manage to absorb his experiences in the world at large and reconcile them with the ordinary daily life of his family. Correspondingly, the parents will normally derive a sense of pleasure and pride from following their child's accounts of his activities at school or work and of his social encounters. Problems will come to the surface and parents should feel relief and reassurance when they learn of these directly from their child. The importance of this open dialogue cannot be emphasised enough. Over recent decades, family life has suffered many changes and we now live days where the work and social commitments of the parents lead to the rarity of occasions when the whole family are sitting together round the same table. Many Jewish families retain the habit of Friday dinners as an important reunion, but this is also becoming a rarity, for endless reasons that outsiders would consider illogical. The family Sunday lunch has simply gone "out of fashion" and this is regrettable. As the teenager moves into university lodgings or finds a job away from home, the setting for family reunions is threatened with extinction. Indeed, this change may lead some parents to experience a sense of liberation, and as long as the adolescent copes with his life away from home, all is well. But if the youngster finds himself in trouble, it may be quite difficult to bring to life the support network that existed when they were all living together.

It is part of normal psychological development that mid- and late-adolescents do not find it easy to approach parents for support when facing some difficult problem. But I believe that, not in spite of, but precisely because of the adolescent's struggles to overcome his resistances, it is the parents who have to ensure that the line of communication with their child remains open. There will be times when a concerned parent's inquiry leads to a response accusing him of being intrusive or of not trusting the adolescent's capacity to look after himself. This is, indeed, painful, but it is still important that the parents should not take this as a closing down of the lines of communication—it is not rare for the same youngster to respond to the next approach with an attitude of spontaneity and pleasure, as if nothing had ever gone wrong between him and the parents.

If the mid- or late-adolescent is suddenly caught in a serious and unexpected crisis, it is likely that he will manage to seek parental support. Presumably, such crises are seen as "accidents", events where the youngster experiences little or no sense of responsibility or guilt, and this will usually make it possible for him to approach his parents for help. But in the course of ordinary life, we have no end of problems that build up in frequency and intensity before reaching a climax. In the majority of these cases, the adolescent will have gone through repeated hesitation about how to deal with what, initially, is not truly seen as a problem—for example, drinking, the use of recreational drugs, sexual adventures, trips that involve missing classes, contact with delinquents, etc. When a "bad habit" or an "exploratory venture" reaches the level of an existential crisis, the adolescent may find it difficult to admit that this has occurred, and the consequence is a struggle to decide who to turn to for help. The youngster will find no end of justifications to explain his reluctance to turn to one or both parents: not wanting to worry them, trying to preserve a sense of self-sufficiency, believing that the problem will be resolved "soon", imagining that the parent(s) will simply condemn him without appreciating his feelings, etc.

Clearly, the degree to which the adolescent hesitates will relate to the prevailing closeness, or distance, between him and his parents. Looking at the parents' side of this picture, we do find parents who either openly or secretly sigh with relief when their child moves out of home and promptly develop a lifestyle where the youngster becomes a visitor; this is, perhaps, unfair, and if the parents' move is accompanied by the message that their "job" of bringing up their child is over, this is both unfair and unkind—in fact, it is dangerous as well. But more often we have parents who believe they must respect their child's independence and their right to privacy, which stops them from contacting the youngster, in case they are seen as intruders or parents who do not believe their child can cope with living away from home. In the vast majority of cases where an adolescent is in trouble and is reluctant to contact his parents, we find that he will blame the parents for creating an insurmountable distance between them—not surprisingly, the parents will virtually repeat these words, blaming their son for pushing them away.

Sex

To what extent can parents influence the sexual development of their children? Turning this question round, to what extent is an individual's sexual development decided by his inborn endowment and what influence will his environment have on this aspect of his life? From the first manifestations of puberty, the youngster has to struggle and learn to live with the changes in his body and with the changes in his feelings about himself and the other people he lives with. Some religions and cultures will impose particular lifestyles, roles, and commitments on the youngster, in line with their preconceptions about how each gender fits into the adopted ethos of that particular group. Statistically, we can assume that the vast majority of adolescents will fall in with parental expectations and demands, but what happens when the youngster finds his impulses taking him into untypical directions?

We live in an era where homosexuality is accepted in most cultures, but if this is true in broad terms, it is still the case that many individuals and families find it difficult to accept this departure from expected norms. In Britain we now have an exceptionally high level of pregnancy in adolescents and it is safe to assume this is a difficult development for both the young woman and for her parents. Statistics now show that tattooing and self-injury have reached a very high level of incidence and, while self-injury is usually kept a secret, tattooing is likely to arouse strong negative feelings in the parents.

In each of these situations it is certain that the adolescent/ young adult sees himself struggling with conflicting sentiments and impulses. What makes these sexual issues particularly serious is the youngster's awareness that each decision will lead to long-term consequences, most of which are, in fact, irreversible. "Identity crises" we call them, and this underlines the interpretation that it is the individual himself who is caught up in a complex struggle with his conscious and unconscious feelings.

But the adolescent or young adult still has to contend with the fact of his involvement with his closest family. If this is not the case, one can only hope that the youngster may have created a supportive network around him. But if he lives with, or is still involved with, his parents, their feelings are likely to play a significant role in these various situations. Some parents may urge their adolescent daughter to seek the termination of a pregnancy, and it is also possible that each parent has a different view on how to proceed. Homosexuality, the youngster "coming out", poses similar challenges. Some parents will simply "disown" their child and this adds a new factor to the youngster's identity crisis.

When the adolescent or young adult departs from the family's views on sexual development, it is virtually axiomatic that the parents take this as a sign of rebellion and react with strong disapproval and hostile challenging words and behaviour. This is perhaps understandable, particularly as it is quite possible that one or both parents may have fought against similar sexual conflicts in their younger years. Nevertheless, ideally, they should take into account that pregnancy, homosexuality, self-injury, hair colouring, unusual clothes and other similar "statements" are external manifestations of existential conflicts that torment the youngster. Considering that some of these produce irreversible consequences, there is the possibility of the youngster regretting his earlier decision and, if this does happens, having parental support is precious.

Mental illness

When a late adolescent or young adult is diagnosed as having a mental disorder, it is likely that he will hope to count on the support of his parents. It is conceivable that some parents will dismiss this diagnosis, protesting against the "medicalisation of human sentiments" and, in some cases, adding that the supposed "mental illness" is no more than the type of personality the youngster has always had. But the precise opposite can also happen, with parents experiencing a sense of relief at discovering that their son's unusual, strange behaviour has been caused by an illness and that, therefore, it may respond to appropriate treatment.

This configuration may appear unlikely or, at least, more difficult, if the youngster's supposed symptoms lead him to strong criticisms of his parents' words or attitudes, present or past. Parents, after all, are also human and they may find it very difficult not to respond to their child's words by taking them at face value. An outsider will recognise that the fact that the youngster throws these accusations at his parents is an indication that, unconsciously, he hopes they will see through the overt meaning and respond to the underlying distress. In other words, the face-to-face verbal attacks on the parents is, paradoxically, an attempt to obtain their understanding and help. A more worrying problem arises when the adolescent/young adult writes off the parents and moves away from them—this leaves no room for the parents to offer any help.

The psychiatrist or therapist may find himself in a difficult situation if his prescribed treatment meets with opposition from the parents of the late adolescent or young adult. Whether drugs or hospitalisation are the doctor's choice, the parents may argue that they can offer help at home to their son or daughter—who may feel quite torn between these conflicting recommendations. It is important that the doctor or therapist bears in mind not so much the true age of the patient, but his actual degree of independence. Not many professionals feel comfortable dealing the parents of young people, but if the patient is emotionally and/or physically dependent on his parents, it is crucial that the professional ensures that himself or another colleague works closely with the parents. A mentally ill adolescent needs more than medication: environmental support is vital for his improvement.

Academic failure

By the time the "normal", average adolescent reaches the ages of seventeen or eighteen, he is usually quite aware of what he would like to do as he moves towards adulthood. Choosing to work in commerce or industry, he will be looking for jobs or seeking training posts to develop his area of expertise. If deciding to follow an academic career, he will be striving to obtain the degrees and pass marks that might enable him to obtain a place at the college or university of his choice.

In the past, it was virtually taken for granted that the late adolescent lived in the parental home until obtaining alternative accommodation at university or as part of his work career. At university, it was likely that he would be studying (and perhaps having accommodation in a students' hall) thanks to a grant. This is no longer the case, and nowadays many parents will have to fund their child's studies. If, instead, he is working or attending a technical course, the parents will in most cases continue to have him living at home.

The parents' occupations will influence their response to the adolescent's doubts and uncertainties in making his choices about the future. Those adolescents whose parents are prepared to voice their views but still allow the youngsters to follow their instincts and experiment with their choices, are lucky; but there will always be parents with very clear views about the adolescent's future who will demand that he conform to these or, if he refuses, will threaten to cut their support off, or actually do so. Ideally, this should never happen, since if he conforms to the demands of the parents, the youngster will, most likely, harbour a deep and lasting resentment, whilst if he decides to rebel against them, he faces a difficult challenge in trying to be self-sufficient.

Ideally, parents should be able to differentiate between a son who wants to defy them and a son who is trying to find a solution to his doubts and fears. Sadly, much too often, a son's struggles are interpreted by parents as defiance or disrespect of their words and sentiments. But this misunderstanding can also occur the other way round, where the parents' wish to help is interpreted by the son as an intrusion and a lack of trust in his abilities. When this is the case and it happens that the adolescent/young adult is in therapy, the therapist may be able to infer from the youngster's account that he *is* misunderstanding the parents, but it can become a delicate technical problem for the therapist to decide whether or not to show the youngster that he is wrong in his depiction of the parents' attitude.

Aggression

You are summoned to the police station because your nineteen-year-old son is accused of hitting and hurting an older person during a street demonstration. How does this make you feel? How do you react? Does it make a difference what the demonstration was about? I am sure you want to believe that your son follows social and political beliefs that are acceptable to you, but it is unlikely that these considerations would make any difference to the authorities. Is hurting an older person significant to you? And what happens if you know (even if the authorities do not) that your son was once suspended from school because of hitting another youngster? Worse still, what if this son has repeatedly tormented his younger siblings?

In theoretical psychoanalytic terms, "aggression" refers to conscious and unconscious feelings, whether these are acted upon or, instead, kept under control, even though influencing the general emotional experience and behaviour of the adolescent. This description follows on from Freud's theories of instincts, where he postulated that humans were endowed with life and death instincts—and "aggression", hostility, was part of the latter. But on a pragmatic level, "aggression" describes physical or verbal attacks that may cause pain to another. However, it is important to appreciate that, even if not acted upon, unconscious aggressive impulses will affect the behaviour and emotional experience of the youngster. For the parents it will make a world of difference whether their son manages to contain his hostile impulses and behave "properly" or, instead, treats those around him as enemies he needs to fight.

In the majority of cases, by the time the adolescent reaches his late teens, the whole family is well aware of his style of dealing with the world around him. But it does happen that a youngster seen as "well-behaved" suddenly acts in violent manner. Sometimes this is "disguised" and displayed in the practice of sports, which is socially acceptable, but whenever the aggressive behaviour is enacted in a manner that causes injury to another person, there is a serious problem for the parents. And here it becomes important to focus on the ethos that these parents have created around the upbringing of their children.

There are families where it simply would never happen that one of the parents would use physical force to show feelings to the spouse or to the children. Similarly, speaking very loudly or shouting when experiencing strong emotions, occurs in some families but not in all. It can be argued that from his earliest days a child learns his family's ways of expressing strong feelings. Indeed, the child will always be punished if resorting to shouting or to physical aggression, but this in itself is a form of teaching that particular child how an older and stronger person can control and punish someone who disobeys his injunctions.

Coming back to our late adolescent who uses physical force in his dealings with other people, the parents' response to this behaviour will depend on their own view of how to deal with aggressive impulses. If we take, for example, a couple where the husband hits out when contradicted or disobeyed, while the wife, though she objects, has accepted it for many years, there is a strong possibility that the son's attacking behaviour will arouse feelings of sympathy and, possibly, pride in the father. But the mother is likely to feel disappointed seeing her son following in his father's footsteps and she may try to find some means of changing the son's behaviour. Whose input will the son accept? The chances are that the son will feel supported by his father, while feeling that the mother is failing to recognise him as an individual in his own right, taking him to be, instead, no more than a copy of his father. And, worse still, we can find that the wife, who has somehow accepted the husband's violence for many years, will take the son's clash with the law as the final straw in the marital relationship and decide to leave.

The situation is very different when the parents are opposed to any form of overt aggression. The son's violence will shock them but, when trying to help him, they must be prepared for statements which they may simply interpret as illogical and nonsensical. The son may claim that their façade of quiet harmony hides considerable hostility and that, whatever they say, fundamentally they are not prepared to see his side of the situation. These assertions should not be corrected or criticised; instead, parents should ask for explanations, getting across the message that they are keen to grasp what has led the son to behave in such a puzzling manner. This approach follows on from the assumption that the adolescent/young adult may be helped to find a different way of dealing with his feelings and impulses.

If the youngster's offence leads to a legal sentence that places him in residential care, parents should try and keep close contact with him. It is important that they convey the message that the youngster has not been written off and that the parental home remains available as a secure haven.

Addictions

In the vast majority of cases, when an adolescent begins to smoke or to use alcoholic drinks, this is linked to having found peers who have introduced him to these habits. By the time he reaches his late teens, he will have turned these activities into an integral part of his position in the world—unless he is one of the few youngsters who manage to avoid turning the experimenting into an addiction. Sadly, not all youngsters possess the capacity to bring reason to bear and to impose self-control to overcome noxious impulses. There are many theories which try to explain the link between smoking and/ or drinking and the person's personality and emotional state. An alternative view is to consider that an addiction, of whatever nature, tends to acquire a life of its own. Indeed, a state of emotional tension or depression may lead the adolescent or young adult to increase his use of smoking or drinking, but it is virtually impossible to explain why self-control and good sense do not come into operation and, instead, a habit is created.

When parents smoke or drink as part of their ordinary lives, they will usually accept their son doing so without much of a fuss. However, in the last few decades, many parents have become anxious about their son either smoking or drinking, because they interpret this as the initial stages of him turning to drugs. And in such cases, the parents' attempt to curb the adolescent's use of alcohol or smoking is likely to create an increasingly intense area of conflict. It is very rare for an adolescent to accept his parents' advice/injunctions in this area. Parents believe they are being moved by love and concern, but the youngster may feel their behaviour is an exaggerated form of intrusion and control. When this happens, the usual and dangerous consequence is the creation of a gap where the adolescent preserves his addiction while trying not to have a definitive break with his parents. This is an extremely delicate situation for the parents, who will often pretend to accept the son's deception in order to preserve the relationship.

If possible, parents should try and avoid a breakdown of the relationship with their son, even when he has gone beyond twenty-years old. The use of alcohol and/or drugs has the potential to trigger life-threatening crises—and parental support in such a situation is precious. If one of the parents has a habit of excessive use of tobacco, alcohol, or other drugs, the son's crisis may produce a clash between the parents, and this makes it even more important that they should try not to allow their conflict to add parental separation to the problems with which their son is struggling.

Crises apart, we now have so many youngsters using alcohol, tobacco, or some kind of drug to varying degrees, that it is important that each family finds its way to establishing some kind of compromise between the parents' view of these habits and the *fact* that their son is using (or abusing) one or more of these drugs. Some families will ask the youngster not to smoke inside the home, while others will demand that when inebriated or intoxicated the son should go straight to his room and avoid potential clashes with parents or siblings. Even when considering these demands to be unfair or discriminating, the vast majority of young adults will accept and comply with them. Sadly, sometimes confrontations errupt and it can be virtually impossible for the parents to act on their knowledge that the son is probably aware that he is behaving irrationally. If possible, once the adolescent or young adult shows clear signs of being intoxicated, the parents should avoid confrontation and, instead, attempt to pacify the son and gradually persuade him to relent and sleep it off.

Handicap

It is safe to assume that no parent manages to approach a handicapped child of his or hers without complex and subtle conflicting feelings. Perhaps these are more easily understood when the handicap is present from birth or early infancy. But even when the handicap is caused by war, illness, or accident in adolescence or adulthood, many parents still feel a sense of guilt for not having provided sufficient protection to their child. Most parents will recognise that this is unrealistic, but they will still find it very difficult to approach the child in a fully objective manner. If they do, some youngsters will find this loving attention gratifying and comforting, but they may still at times resent being "treated as an incompetent baby".

Having a child born with a physical or psychological handicap demands from the parents a long and complex process of adjustment. Ideally, both parents should share their feelings and offer each other much-needed support. Complications can arise when the handicap is attributed to some hereditary factor in one of the parents or, as has been established in recent years, when the handicap is attributed to the mother's habits during pregnancy. The resulting conflict may well require professional help, in order that the child is not deprived of the care he needs.

Adolescence and adulthood will pose difficult problems for the handicapped individual—and for his parents. We now have legal battles over demands for sterilisation of handicapped adolescent young women. Even when living in specialised sheltered accommodation, handicapped youngsters will usually be counting on parental support, and it is most important that professionals address the needs of both patient and parents.

Adoption

It is usually in late adolescence that adopted children tend to question their sense of belonging and their position in the world. Children adopted at a very early age tend to grow up quite happily with their parents, whether they are aware or not that these are not their biological parents. There have been endless discussions about the best age at which to tell the child he has been adopted. In practice, it is very difficult to know whether this information serves the child's needs or those of the parents. Some children will turn a deaf ear to this revelation, and it is true that some children become immensely distressed by finding that what they thought was a certainty has suddenly turned into a lie.

Reaching late teens, the adolescent begins to compare (consciously and unconsciously) his developing sexual self with the image he has built up of the parents with whom he has grown up. If one of the parents is the object of negative, critical, hostile feelings, this can lead to serious, unpleasant confrontations. Perhaps he would behave in exactly the same way if this were his biological parent, but being adopted, the adolescent is also struggling with feelings of blame that the parent has "taken him away" from his real parents. In such a situation, the parent in question tends to feel enormously hurt and rejected, particularly if adoption was originally seen as a kind of rescuing.

Many parents find it very difficult to cope with a barrage of accusations and, sometimes, threats. And yet it is vital that he or she manages to struggle to keep open the communication with the adolescent or young adult. Real breakdown occurs when the adolescent or young adult decides to cut his ties with his parents and disappears from home. As long as the youngster is there—even if he is continuously throwing accusations at the parent—there is hope, and it is important to respond to the youngster.

Another problem can occur when an adopted adolescent becomes homosexual. Indeed, this definition of sexual orientation will result from multiple factors, but when the particular youngster was adopted it is *possible* that this choice might be influenced by a conscious or unconscious wish not to inflict on a newborn the kind of problems that the adopted youngster believes children can go through. Parents can experience this turn of events as an accusation and attempt to convince the youngster that he is moving in the wrong direction. It is most unlikely that the youngster will engage in such discussions, but whatever their views, it is important that the adoptive parents do not disown their child.

Many, if not most of us, are accustomed to causal thinking, and when focusing on an adopted youngster it is very easy to find ourselves, sooner or later, attributing that youngster's life decisions to the fact of his being adopted. Indeed, that is what his parents will do all the time, but as professionals, it is important to keep an open mind and remain aware of the difference between hypothesis and fact. When seeing parents who blame themselves for their youngster's problems, we should attempt to draw their attention to other possible factors that might equally be seen as viable explanations of his words or behaviour.

Summing up

At the end of the day, how much influence can a parent truly have on his or her child once he reaches late adolescence and adulthood? Many parents seem able to feel their "job is done" after their child reaches late teens and, indeed, they may move home or even transfer to another city or country, apparently happy to rely on modern means of communication to sustain some degree of contact with their youngster. But many other parents remain keen to preserve a close contact with their children. Some want to become grandparents and ensure the continuity of the family across the generations. Other parents may have formed close conscious or unconscious links with a particular child and this will lead them to try very hard to keep an intimate relation with the adolescent/adult child.

As in many, or all, other human areas, prediction is impossible. Even a retrospective assessment, where one might claim the wisdom of hindsight, still leaves room for conflicting interpretations, particularly when a parent and a child are involved. In spite of all this, it is safe to assume that every single individual values the interest of another person, particularly that of a parent. If interest is blended with sympathy and empathy, this will be valued, whatever the overt response of the adolescent/young adult.

If having a child is a choice the parents have made, it should follow that at no time should they forget, or give up, their commitment to support that child. It must be assumed that, whatever his words or behaviour, the child (irrespective of his age) knows that it is the parents who have brought him up—and he will value the parents for not having written him off.

References

Erikson, E. (1965). *Childhood and Society*. London: The Hogarth Press.

Freud, A. (1972). Child analysis as a sub-speciality of psychoanalysis. *International Journal of Psychoanalysis, 53*: 151–156.

Freud, A. (1936). Normality and pathology. In: *The Ego and the Mechanisms of Defence* (p. 170). London: The Hogarth Press, 1966.

Freud, A. (1958). Adolescence. In: *Psychoanalytic Study of the Child, 13*: 255–278.

Freud, S. (1905). Three Essays on the Theory of Sexuality. *S. E. 7*: 207.

Musil, R. (2001). *The Confusions of Young Törless*. London: Penguin Classics.

Segal, H. (1972). The role of child analysis in the general psychoanalytical training. In: *International Journal of Psychoanalysis, 53*: 157–161.

Stern, D. (1995). *The Motherhood Constellation*. New York: Basic Books.

Winnicott, D. (1965). Adolescence: struggling through the doldrums. In: *The Family and Individual Development*. London: Tavistock publications.

INDEX

93